TOM DAWE

NEW AND COLLECTED

TOM DAWE

NEW AND COLLECTED POEMS

BREAKWATER
P.O. BOX 2188, ST. JOHN'S, NL, CANADA, A1C 6E6
WWW.BREAKWATERBOOKS.COM

EDITOR: James Langer
COVER PHOTO: Ray Fennelly

ISBN 978-1-55081-755-3

A CIP catalogue record for this book is available from Library and Archives Canada

We acknowledge the support of the Canada Council for the Arts. We acknowledge the financial support of the Government of Canada and the Government of Newfoundland and Labrador through the Department of Tourism, Culture, Industry and Innovation for our publishing activities.
PRINTED AND BOUND IN CANADA.

Canada Council for the Arts Conseil des arts du Canada
Canada
Newfoundland Labrador
ArtsNL
NEWFOUNDLAND AND LABRADOR ARTS COUNCIL

Breakwater Books is committed to choosing papers and materials for our books that help to protect our environment. To this end, this book is printed on a recycled paper that is certified by the Forest Stewardship Council®.

FSC www.fsc.org
RECYCLED
Paper made from recycled material
FSC® C103567

To my friends Jean Pierre Andrieau, Melvin Baker, Gerald Barnable, Tom Burke, Sean Connors, Paul Heneghan, Andrew Hutton, John Lewis, Kevin Melvin, Gerry Penney, Ron Whelan, Bob Woodland, and Bruce Woodland

And in memory of Aidan Maloney, Paul O'Neill, and Gerry Squires

ACKNOWLEDGEMENTS

Tom Dawe's first full-length collection, *Hemlock Cove and After*, was published by Breakwater in 1975. A small collection of previously published poems, entitled *In a Small Cove*, was printed by Wychwood Press (U.K.) in 1978. *Island Spell* appeared in 1981, published by Harry Cuff Publications. A new and selected poems, *In Hardy Country*, was published by Breakwater in 1993. *Where Genesis Begins* appeared from Breakwater in 2009 and featured Dawe's poetry alongside the work of renowned visual artist Gerald Squires (1937-2015) with a foreword by Martina Seifert and afterword by Stan Dragland. *Hemlock Cove and After* and *Island Spell* included illustrations by the author.

The collection *Pilgrim* is published here for the first time. The poem "Remembering Leonard" appeared in *Gift of Silence: A Haiku Tribute to Leonard Cohen* (*Editions des petits nuages*, 2018). The author extends gratitude to ArtsNL for their financial support during the completion of *Pilgrim.*

The section of uncollected poems presented in this volume is not exhaustive as it contains only those works, from various sources, permitted for inclusion by the author: "The Sculpin" from *Newfoundland Quarterly (*1965); "Dog-Fish Summer" from a Newfoundland Arts and Letters Prize booklet (1968); "Apparition," "Feathers," "Snow-Poem Suggestion," and "Summer of Forty

Something-or-Other" appeared in the Canadian literary journal *Other Voices* between 1968 and 1972; "A Farewell to Arms" *Scruncheons* (journal) 1972; "Children From Porlock," "Gulls and Ice," "Monday Morning," "Ottawa October Crisis, 1970," and "Summer Was" from *Connections* (Memorial University, 1972), a shared collection with poet Tom Moore; "Evening, Signal Hill" from *Quarry* (1973); "In There Somewhere" and "On the Full Tide" from *31 Newfoundland Poets*, edited by Adrian Fowler and Al Pittman (Breakwater 1979); "In the Heart of the Country," "Leah," "Sole Survivor," "The Signs," and "Haiku Selection" were composed in the early eighties and are previously unpublished.

By the late eighties, Dawe's first two collections were long out of print, so he began revising and republishing some of the earlier poems in subsequent collections. Only the last published versions are preserved here, and they appear within their most recent sequences. To assist with locating the antecedents of Dawe's revised work, the appendix provides the original table of contents from each of the poet's first three collections.

The editor thanks Tom Dawe (for his graciousness and warmhearted wisdom), K, RM, and the staff of the QEII Library at Memorial University.

CONTENTS

Pilgrim (2019)

19 TREK
20 TOMMY
21 TO MARY OLIVER
22 VISITATION
23 FLORENCE HARDY
24 AQUARIUS
25 AT L'ANSE AUX MEADOWS
26 WITNESS
27 BONFIRE
28 CHARLIE BROWN
30 CHRISTMAS EVE
31 CIRCUS
33 COUNTRY SONG
34 CROWS
35 DEVIL
37 FINAL
38 FEBRUARY WINDOW
39 THE WAY
40 AFTER GEORGIA O'KEEFFE
41 VIVALDI
42 BIRDS AND POETS
43 GHOST STORY

44 ISLAND WOMAN
45 NIGHT CLASS
46 AFTER RAIN
47 WATERCOURSE
48 HAWK SONG
49 IN THE HAPPILY EVER AFTER
51 OF MICE AND BOOKS
54 JACOB
55 GRAND CANYON
56 ONLY THE WIND
57 MAKE-AND-BREAK
59 ON LEARNING THAT WE SHARE 99% OF OUR DNA WITH LETTUCE
60 OLD BELIEVER
61 PEGASUS
62 FAMILY
64 REMEMBERING LEONARD
65 PILGRIM
66 PATH'S END
67 SANTA FE TRAIL
68 NORTH LIGHT
69 VIKING SITE
70 TO WILLIAM CARLOS WILLIAMS
71 TWELFTH NIGHT
72 THE GROVE
73 GOD'S DOG
75 OTTERS ON ALL SOUL'S DAY
76 LOON
78 SEARCHING FOR ANCESTORS

Where Genesis Begins (2009)

83 ALL TO OURSELVES
86 BESS

89 THOREAU
91 DARWIN
92 ELSEWHERE: A POEM TO EMILY
95 COFFIN MAKER
97 GNOSTIC
98 CAT POEM
99 MY CAT IN NOAH'S ARK
100 FROG-PRINCE
101 MAN OF LETTERS
102 FLEA
103 THE SHOP
105 RIGGS
107 SALMON
108 AFTER THE STORM
109 TEA ROOM
110 COWBOYS
112 HANSEL AND GRETHEL
114 CHILD ON MICHAELMAS
116 ASTERS
118 SALTBOX HOUSE
120 SOLOMON KANE
121 LOT'S WIFE
123 NERO
124 CALIGULA'S HORSE
126 HOBO BILL
128 PAGES
129 XANTIPPE
130 HERMIT
131 NEW YEAR'S MORNING, 2000
133 SLIPS
135 THE LAST KEEPER
137 THE SECOND WIFE
139 THE LAST HOUSE
140 GOAT AND APPLE TREE
142 FOGSCAPE

from In Hardy Country (1993)

147 IN HARDY COUNTRY
149 A FAIRY TALE
151 RIDDLE
153 STILL LIFE
155 DEVIL AT THE DANCE
156 THE BOGEY MAN
158 SOLSTICE, OUTPORT CHILDHOOD
159 UNCLE
160 PEPPERMINT ROCK
162 ONE FALL NIGHT
163 OUTPORT CHRISTMAS
164 ON SMALL ISLAND
165 BOATMAN
167 CARETAKER
169 A DAY IN '45
170 THE DEAD BOY
171 SUMMERPLACE
172 ABANDONED OUTPORT
173 AT WESTERN ARM
174 DARK MORNING
175 THE MUMMER
177 THE OLD MAN AND THE MOON
178 FIGURES FROM ANCESTRAL LANDSCAPE
179 THE BEAR
182 COMMUNION
183 EVENING, BARENEED, CONCEPTION BAY
184 THE WATCHER
185 THE NAKED MAN
187 THE WIDOW AND THE BUTCHER BOY
189 PEGGY
191 MARSH
192 VORTEX

193 CAPE SHORE WOMAN
198 STAGE
199 TOP OF THE WORLD
201 A CONSECRATION
202 IN A SMALL COVE
203 THE FRENCH SHORE MAN
205 BONFIRE NIGHT
206 THE BALLAD OF FLORA
208 IN PICASSO'S "MADMAN"
210 HAIKU (1)
211 HAIKU (2)
212 HAIKU (3)
213 HAIKU (4)
214 HAIKU (5)
215 ON CUSLETT BROOK (1979)
216 EDWARDIANS (OLD PHOTOGRAPH)
217 BACK ROAD
219 THE VETERAN (1)
220 THE VETERAN (2)
221 WILD GEESE
223 SANDPIPER
224 IF SONNETS WERE IN FASHION
226 "STRUGGLE INTO LIGHT": A POEM TO JOHN CLARE
229 ALDERS
230 METHODISTS
232 BITCH
234 CALLING THE CHILDREN
235 DAEDALUS
238 DAEDALUS AT GARDEN WALL
240 SEABIRD
241 HIDE AND SEEK

from Island Spell (1981)

247 GHOSTS

249 THE FAR ISLAND

250 THE POTATO GROUND

252 INTERVAL

253 ONCE BY THE ATLANTIC

255 THE SCYTHE

258 WHITE HORSES

259 THE GUITAR PLAYER

261 ALONG THAT COAST

263 THE STRANGER

265 THREE IN THE SUMMER AFTERNOON

266 ISHMAEL REMEMBERS (1)

267 ISHMAEL REMEMBERS (2)

269 THE BRIDGE

271 BEACH MOMENTS, SEPTEMBER '56

272 THE HEADLAND

273 THE VETERAN (3)

274 LOW TIDE

275 POOR PETER

277 ONCE AFTER SUNDAY

278 TO A POET

from Hemlock Cove and After (1975)

283 INUK

289 STRANGER AT HEMLOCK COVE

298 THE TRAPPER

300 THE CELLAR

301 ISHMAEL

302 FROM THE LIGHTHOUSE

303 SCAPE

304 NOAH

305 HOUSE ON THE COAST

306 SCARECROW
307 STORM COMING, WINTER AFTERNOON
309 DREAMING OF AN ALMOST FORGOTTEN FRIEND
310 THE ANGLER
311 CONNECTIONS
312 TRIP
313 THE MADONNA
324 SOMETHING GONE
327 BY THE TRACKS
326 BIRTH CONTROL
327 CHILDREN IN THE ALLEY
328 THE LITTLE MAN
329 BABEL

Uncollected (1965–1985)

333 THE SCULPIN
337 DOG-FISH SUMMER
343 APPARITION
344 FEATHERS
345 SNOW-POEM SUGGESTION
346 A FAREWELL TO ARMS
347 CHILDREN FROM PORLOCK
348 OTTAWA OCTOBER CRISIS, 1970
349 MONDAY MORNING
350 GULLS AND ICE
351 SUMMER WAS
352 SUMMER OF FORTY SOMETHING-OR-OTHER
353 EVENING, SIGNAL HILL
354 IN THERE SOMEWHERE
356 ON THE FULL TIDE
358 IN THE HEART OF THE COUNTRY
360 LEAH
362 SOLE SURVIVOR
363 THE SIGNS

364 HAIKU SELECTIONS
WEST COUNTRY CEMETERY
AFTER BEETHOVEN
AGAIN THE OWL...
ABANDONED LIGHTHOUSE
AFTER KAZANTZAKIS
LONG AFTER
MISTY TWILIGHT
SUSPENDED
IMAGINING
GOOD FRIDAY

375 APPENDIX: ORIGINAL CONTENTS
379 INDEX OF FIRST LINES
387 INDEX OF TITLES

2019

PILGRIM

"I believe a leaf of grass
is no less than
the journey-work
of the stars"

—WALT WHITMAN

TREK

alone on the barrens
I trek in the eye
of the hidden fox

fern music
fiddleheads becoming
fairy pipes

surprised
by the shyness
of a lady's slipper

catch and release—
blood and rainbow
on my hands

call of unknown bird
          something
I'm not wild enough
          to answer

TOMMY

Tommy, the hermit,
started turning up in public,
especially at wakes
in the new funeral home
where plenty of food was sure
to be on the table.

Like the uninvited fairy
at a christening,
he became a disturbance,
a nagging nemesis of sorts,
the reddleman of his ancestors,
earth and stable
pungent on his clothes.

Eventually, for the sake of a snack
and a strong cup of tea,
he sniffed mortality everywhere,
like the time he shocked my mother
by asking if she was
soon going to die.

With apologies to Eliot
and his Prufrock,
it could be said
that Tommy measured
out our lives
with tea
and coffee spoons.

TO MARY OLIVER

precious pagan
the fish you caught
becoming you

offshore
herring take flight
as gannets

flowers rise
from dark spots
where the vulture fed

otter imagines
the river
lasting forever

Buddha
frog unblinking
in a ditch

in a world
always
being born

wondering
what the creatures
really know

VISITATION

Out from a droke of woods
a shadow crosses the yard,
stable clapboards and chicken coop.

> Grandfather, a study in grey,
> struggles
> to stuff a muzzleloader.
> Mother keeps us indoors.
> Like a Good Friday sadness
> or blinds pulled down
> while something passes.

Sea wind under a porch door,
and somewhere outside,
real as caplin rotting,
the death angel
perched in a dogberry tree
waiting.

FLORENCE HARDY

Sometimes I imagine you
and the old poet
under the sheets,
back to back,
long after midnight,
mute in the immensity
of a cold Wessex bed.
He, fiddling back
his dead Emma
and all the girls
he loved once
from a distance
at fairs and country dances.
And you, waiting out another night,
in that museum of a house
you never liked,
listening to the wind slap
wet flaccid leaves
against windowpanes.

Sad to fancy you there
silently calling back scripture,
imagining yourself
a dutiful, young Abishag
warming an old king's bed,
reaching out timidly
in the ticking darkness
to touch the frail, bony body
that once belonged
to a shepherd boy.

AQUARIUS

In our hippie days
we thought we had Zen down pat,
beggars without bowls

by the gateless gate,
nourished on wordless sermons.
In our hippie days,

crazy for koans,
we were all philosophers
and natural poets.

On the way not sought,
enlightened in the here and now,
we thought the body

would soon drop away,
but the body reminded us
that love was free.

In sweet summer grass,
the rustle of four hands
as we undressed each other,

drowned out
the sound
of one hand
clapping.

AT L'ANSE AUX MEADOWS

It happened at the Viking site one afternoon
in a sliver of August chill:
To tourists around a fire
inside a sod house,
the local interpreter
hovering in smoke,
a man in a Parks Canada jacket,
suddenly became more intriguing
than anything Viking.

Bending to put sticks on the fire,
he happened to mention something
about wood for the winter.
And, just like that,
they were all curious about the local customs.
For a few minutes,
answering their questions,
he was the Northman,
great axe in hand,
surviving there all year round
in a tiny village
at the top of the world.

WITNESS

In many and various ways, creators
have been always telling us to pay attention...
pay attention...
from ancients to Updike,
who said that, without us, the universe would be
unwitnessed,
not really there at all.

Consider the Buddha,
his wordless sermon,
that day under a tree, his followers around him,
when he smiled and directed their attention
to the flower in his hand.

Georgia O'Keeffe, a voice from the desert,
said that, because nobody really sees a flower,
she would paint it big, exaggerate,
surprise us into taking time
to see.

And, reading between lines of scripture,
God is always
in another wilderness,
re-stressing holiness in the commonplace.
Like a celestial curmudgeon,
complaining that he has
to set the bush on fire
to make Moses
and the rest of us see.

BONFIRE

It was the last place he wanted to be that night,
Father, mad as hell, out in the wind on a potato patch.
But it was Guy Fawkes Night and Mother was determined
my brother and I should have our first bonfire.
He swore savagely, bending, going down on all fours
to claw dry stalks together with his bare hands.
At the wood's edge he reached up. His big axe struck
a couple of spruce limbs down from the sky.
Soon the small pile was flaming brightly. Sparks flew
on the wind. It didn't last long but we were satisfied.
He said nothing on the way back.

Tonight, all those years later, I'm in November again.
Fellow workers and I, nine months on strike,
are tending an oil-drum fire outside a wire fence.
Gazing pensively into the glow sometimes,
I see the old man in a flicker, still scowling,
and, dear God, I'm remembering the words
I said to myself that night, about when I grew up
I'd have a fire every night if I wanted to.

CHARLIE BROWN

Who could be
more human,
more misunderstood,
more all of us than you?

You, sad and bullied,
yet stoic
in the savage democracy
of the schoolyard.

Always you,
with the game lost,
in there in relief,
when they made fun
at your moon countenance,
your pie face,
your beach-ball head.
You in the simple frame,
fellow of few lines
in very ordinary
complex
not-much-said.

When tomboy Patty
asked if you'd like
to have been
Abraham Lincoln,
you replied
it was hard enough
just being
plain
Charlie Brown.

II

Who said
comic strips
were just
for kids?

Snoopy enters,
crossing the field,
sneering.
What could make
a fellow feel
more insignificant
and alone
in the universe
than having his dog
line up
on the other side?

CHRISTMAS EVE

solitary walk
trying again
to be acquainted
with the night

memories
of village
in a glass ball
paperweight

a child's nativity
animals inside halo
around baby
wise men
outside

nostalgic thoughts
but something
tilts the globe

approaching suburbia
too many lights
for stars

raffle bells
neon Santa
on and off
above traffic

deepening snowfall
soleprints
to parking lot
where stable
used to be

CIRCUS

I remember the year
the circus came and stayed.
An August northeaster
rocked the Ferris wheel,
carrying off the pony tent,
leaving the scrawny creatures
to forage on the commons.

It was the summer
the balloon man
released all his balloons,
took a bus to St. John's
and never came back.
Without his paint and feathers,
the white "Indian" became
one of my uncle's drinking buddies.

On all fours, we children
would elude the ticket-master.
Like rodents, we were everywhere.
One day I spied on
a drunken clown,
stamping his mask into the mud
when the fortune teller told him
she was pregnant.

In a tent half a mile away,
night after sultry night,
a travelling preacher roared
that we were all sinners,
his hell more gruesome
than any Bosch painting.

II

That summer the radio
brought unsettling news from St. John's
about a leftover Victorian character
named Spring-Heeled Jack.
A woman claimed she saw him
one night on Water Street,
leaping clear over the roof
of the Steers premises.

And word came from Placentia Bay
of terrible water-bulls,
horned creatures
from the shadows
of Irish mythology,
looking up from the bottom
at frightened lobster fishermen.

Meanwhile, in a house,
at the end of our lane,
the first television set appeared.
Never again would the front room
be just for wakes and weddings.
We clustered there, patiently,
staring at the magic box,
waiting for the big show,
gawking at the black-and-white
Indigenous chief
in the center
of a test-pattern.

COUNTRY SONG

In a saltbox house under February stars,
Uncle Jake, the oldest man at the spree,
sang a country song up at the top of the stairs
where nobody slept.
I'd never heard him sing before.
I was a catcher in the crowd,
a child peeping in,
just finding out what a wedding was.
I dreaded that room where ghosts clung to coat hangers,
goblins hobnobbed in mothballs
and a broom in a corner waited for a witch.
Uncle Jake sang country,
quavering, faltering, off-key sometimes,
slipping into chin music when he forgot the words.
As the bottle was passed around,
he gave Eddie Arnold a damn good run for his roses.

Uncle Jake sang country.
It was worthy of a notch in the beam.
Others were chiming in.
I laughed aloud. I swayed to the tune.
Something special was happening,
an exorcism of sorts.
I was no longer afraid.
The room grew brighter, cosy as the kitchen.
The tumblers clinking just for me.

CROWS

one for sorrow
two for joy

three for a girl
four for a boy

a ring
of voices
chanting
in a schoolyard

sun scudding
echoes
from steep cliffs

suddenly
a footnote
to the old rhyme—

how playful
the crow
and its shadow

DEVIL

I

Years ago, before I knew
yin and yang fitted into each other,
or John Milton tried to justify
the ways of God to man,
I asked the wrong question in Sunday School:
If Heaven was a perfect place,
why did war break out up there,
with Lucifer and his angels all kicked out?

II

Lord of the Underworld, in from a dung pile,
Lord of the Flies. Yet Lord of the glistening air.
And don't forget the garden. He's there, fairy man,
with his darning needle...horse stinger,
shoelander, dragonfly. He could be
the buzz heard by Emily Dickenson, as she died.

III

Most feared Rumpelstiltskin,
lone mummer, perfect on a tin whistle,
riddler on the soul's road,
figure from an almost forgotten ballad.
If he asks you to name him,
"old fellow" is nice and would suffice.

IV

I'm ten summers young, pushing a wheelbarrow,
door to door with fish to sell. And flies buzzing.
Seems nobody wants to buy the haddock.
I'm confronting the legend,

from gill to tail, the mark of his fingernail
across the slimy skin.

V

Lover as shapeshifter. Something
"very bad" coming down the road.
Handsome fellow on horseback asking
(see Yeats) a woman to go riding with him.
When she refuses, he vanishes.
Another time, he appears to a woman
as sheets of paper blowing in the wind.
Suddenly he's a young man
asking her to go walking.
She too refuses, and, just like that,
he's not there anymore.
Will a third visitation
complete the story?

VI

In Robert Bly's "Snow Banks North of the House,"
the man in the black coat turns
at the end of the road. Like a figure once
in my aunt's nightmare,
a family ghost story handed down.
Followed by the stranger in a long, dark coat,
she runs into the merchant's house,
peering through the window as he goes by.
He turns and looks back at her.
A gargoyle glance.
Nobody speaks. The figures behind her,
the merchant's family are all manikins.
The clock has stopped. It's cold
and the fire is out.

FINAL

biology lab
stray raindrops
tadpole down
window glass

catching myself
dreaming
in a final exam

diagrams
duly rendered
facts remembered
blanks filled in

how ancient
the pond
in a frog's
indifferent eye

Basho's diminished
green man
dissected
on a slab

never again
to plunge
into the sound
of water

FEBRUARY WINDOW

musing
on differences
between soul
and spirit

I am struck
suddenly
by the brown-golden
medieval moment
of nine shrivelled apples
still clinging
to their boughs

and then a squirrel
seal-like
in deep snow
frisky
with an apple
on its nose

THE WAY

abandoned cove
the cobbler's shop
lopsided
in snow flurries

faint trail
of sprigs
mouse tracks
on frozen floor

the way
birch
taps
grey shingles

AFTER GEORGIA O'KEEFFE

close-up
surprised
by the physics
of flowers

dark riddle
at edge
of morning-glory

all those erotic
caves
that suck you in

horse skull
ghost rider
on desert sky

bare bones alive
  something Ezekiel
  in the dry valley

VIVALDI

after your "Summer"
a fly buzzing
scores
the silence

lifting a window
half-expecting
your bird note
imitations

just the sound
of dust
settling

after
woodpecker's
tapping

BIRDS AND POETS

Thomas Hardy:
lost Wessex
childhood
when nightingales sang
near a bedroom window.

Edward Thomas:
in a sad pause
on a battlefield
the song
of an unknown bird.

Mary Oliver:
a rare thrush
music
too wonderful
to be with us always.

Winter morning:
a lot depends also
on a stranded robin
silent
as I chop wood.

GHOST STORY

Experts will point out, correctly, that the Beothuk
didn't use horses. But, aside from fact and footnote,
old stories linger on, waiting us out,
making us servants to the telling.
It's said that if you stay all night
on a certain deserted island in Notre Dame Bay,
somewhere before dawn, on a low wind,
you'll hear faint hoof-beats going by.
Next morning, explore all you like,
daylight will reveal nothing from the night before.

I've stayed on the island myself, amazed
at how small and confined the place is.
Hard to imagine a settlement ever existed there
or a house in which the last white settler was waked
with coppers on his eyes.

How numinous landwash can be,
especially in summer twilight
when owls in the dark spruce
ask questions.

ISLAND WOMAN

I don't know how we stood it all. Childhood was all work,
drudgery.
The Sabbath was our only day off
and that was for dwelling on our sins.
We were told the angels wrote them down.
It was even a sin to sew a stitch on that day
or use the scissors. They might stick to our fingers.
No wonder I was afraid of my shadow.

Put yourself in my place, a little girl called out of bed before
daylight
to help catch the sheep for the boat to Fogo.
My teeth chattered under the full moon
as I chased the black one.
But something wasn't right , the others were calling out,
laughing at me. How foolish I must have looked.
You see, there was no black sheep at all.
There I was, stumbling around on the frosty grass, half-asleep,
chasing a white ram's shadow.

NIGHT CLASS

FOR GERARD COLLINS

I'd just finished my lecture on Conrad,
Marlow's Congo voyage, far, far in,
a shocking journey into self,
when a sad-faced young fellow came up to say
that he was probably quitting the class.
"Too many old people," he said, shyly.
Several minutes later,
another student, an older woman,
approached me to say
that this night slot was likely not for her.
"Too many young people," she said.

AFTER RAIN

listening
at open window
as something
small-winged
brushes by

downwind
from honeysuckle—
all the summers
I've been in

a bittern's call—
lost ponds
I'll never see
again

WATERCOURSE

shards of sea glass—
          morning message
          outside bottle

aspen streams
      seep up from
            sleep of trilobites

         the duck's own way
      on rivers
in the sky

HAWK SONG

in a poem
about Blake dying
Mary Oliver declares:

"When a man says
he hears angels singing,
he hears angels singing."

I wonder what
she would have said
about my mother

an old woman
sitting on a back porch
rejoicing
in her last summer

claiming
that a hawk
was singing.

IN THE HAPPILY EVER AFTER

Rumpelstiltskin will remain,
moving to and fro in the earth.
Only his compatriots
will be permitted to call him "Rump."
Sticks and stones
won't break his bones,
only the name will break him...
for the time being.

Unable to forget the hairy fellow
in her grandmother's nightdress,
Riding Hood will discard her hoodie
and stop walking in the woods.
She'll grow up and become
a university folklore major
focusing on grim tales
from the far north
where the grandmother herself
is sometimes the monster
trying to devour
her grandchildren.

Jack will be a sucker
for the next trader
coming down the road.
He'll grow bored
with the giant's singing harp.
As for the special hen,
he'll feel it's too old-fashioned

to be bartering eggs at the store,
gold ones or not.
And he'll never again
use a row of beans
as a figure of speech.

II

Sleeping Beauty will suffer
from chronic insomnia,
unlike the royal husband
snoring beside her.
Night after night, she'll ponder sadly
the lost possibility of being
kissed by a stranger,
some woodcutter, hunter or berry-picker,
breaking through the briars.

OF MICE AND BOOKS

At a garage sale this morning,
picking through piles of books,
noticing a spine-broken edition
of Bacon's essays,
I realize he could have been
referring to mice
when he wrote that
some books are to be tasted,
others to be swallowed,
and some few
to be chewed
and digested.

I see evidence everywhere.
Mice love and thoroughly
gobble Dr. Seuss,
chew fondly on mini volumes
of Beatrix Potter
and wolf down E.B. White.
Their favourite poet
is Robbie Burns
who showed empathy
for their species long ago.
With gusto they feast
on Steinbeck's Mice and Others.
But pickings are few.

They scurry in the dust,
scampering around the walls
of Troy and *Middlemarch*
without a nibble,
sniffing at Plato's dialogues,

curious, perhaps,
about that cave
he talked about.

II

For mice, holiness is
a foreign concept,
wisdom books and apologetics
are not to their taste.
The musine conscience
is never bothered
by dust on the Bible.
They ignore Jane Austen,
blissfully unaware
that she's made a palatable comeback
in our time
and some humans still peruse her
for the sake of balanced sentences.

Except for an occasional
munched-up Huck,
mice appear to be bored
with on-the-road novels.
They and their ilk
were picaresque
long before us.
They've no appetite for

the Hemingway hero,
since grace under pressure
is old hat to a mouse.

They've dropped
pointed comments
of their own:
little pinched colons,
a spatter of crappy commas
and full plops.

JACOB

northern dawn
how ghostly the white
crab blossoms

familiar in daylight
last night's dead
birch
was ladder
to the stars

I have wrestled
all night
with a poem

GRAND CANYON

Don Marquis once said
that publishing a book of poetry
is like dropping a rose petal
down the Grand Canyon
and waiting for the echo.
I've been there.
And, to other poets,
I remind you, as I remind myself,
how wonderful the Canyon can be.
Consider your choices:
all those small, branching paths
leading down.

Along earth's tally-stick,
may you pick up what the river says,
and arrive at the playful side
of raven's shadow.
May you be struck
by the cascading song
of the Canyon wren,
and rose fragrance
rising
on an Anasazi wind.

ONLY THE WIND

FOR R. L. S.

Your nurse whispered
it was only the wind
when you questioned
sounds in the night,

up from a child's sleep
to a horseman outside,
galloping on the rain.

Only the wind, you were told,
not convinced at all
as years shadowed past,

and you coughed up blood
on your land of counterpane.
Later in your brief life

you brought the horseman back,
gave him a poem
in your *Garden of Verses*,
for children, they said.

But you tended that garden
for the child
within,

in the spirit
of Tolkien, perhaps,
in a new century,
when he said
there was no such thing
as writing for children.

MAKE-AND-BREAK

At my father's wake, men talked
of the strength in his arms,
how, hand on the tiller, he could bend
and trip the wheel from the stern of the skiff.
Just a flick of the wrist, they said.
I watched some of his friends at the casket,
caressing the wood, declaring it primed
for the voyage.
I never saw him as a boatman at all,
more farmer than fisherman
in his West Country blood.
But he always seemed to be going somewhere
in search of parts for a decrepit
make-and-break engine.

In 1979 I went with him one last time
out to the Cape Shore looking for an engine.
That day he seemed sad, out of sorts,
when fog rolled in.
He thought he saw a village in the distance
and tried to point it out to me.
I laughed when it turned out to be
just cattle grazing on a bog.

A few nights ago in a dream
we were together again
on the road to Point Lance
in a shroud of fog.
I laughed, reminding him

of the day we saw the cattle.
But he told me to look closer.

And this time it was really a village,
strange and familiar
at the same time.
As we approached the houses,
I knew for sure that a widow there
had an engine to sell.

ON LEARNING THAT WE SHARE 99% OF OUR DNA WITH LETTUCE

This has existential implications. Seriously, such negligible
difference between us and a tossed salad. I must celebrate,
rejoice at my place in the web of things, even though
the spider waits.
My deep sense of otherness in the universe will diminish.
I'll turn down the lights, making it easier
for the fairies to come back.

Still, it's sobering to imagine myself an old fellow,
getting carried away with all this,
wandering among my kin in the vegetable aisles
of the supermarket, tickling turnip tops,
cavorting with cucumbers, collards and kale.
After the Loblaw's police have led me away,
the written report will state I was observed
looking under cabbage leaves,
conversing with a cauliflower,
poking green peppers
and singing to the spinach.

OLD BELIEVER

She believes in God,
single-parent Almighty,
best-selling author,
King James version only.
When you tell her you're puzzled
by the Book of Revelations,
she counts you among the lost,
scorning your spiritual blindness
and lack of discernment.
Fervent as any ancient zealot,
she's got it in for the Romans,
especially the Catholic ones.
Her Jesus is decidedly brass-knuckled,
bloody, a stern-faced fighter
for the Good.
She longs for that blessed day
when he'll ride back,
no longer on a little donkey.
Supreme military commander,
sword in his fist,
he'll set everything straight.
Smug among the saved,
she swoons at the thought
of a bloody battle,
an Armageddon
to end it all,
and one lovely hell
of a lesson
for the rest of us.

PEGASUS

My mother, who grew up on a farm, had an explanation
for her fear of horses,
and her recurring nightmare,
a Fuseli version with wide nostrils and glowing eyes:
It all went back to a dusty day in childhood
when she was knocked unconscious
by the hooves of a runaway.

Later in her life the nightmare faded.
She started to look back nostalgically,
even writing verse about countryside left behind.
And one night the dream horse returned,
glistening, ghostly, more terrible than ever, she said,
on powerful, great beating wings.

FAMILY

A POET LAUREATE'S GREETING TO NEW CANADIANS,
ST. JOHN'S, JUNE, 2012

Back in the Romantic Age,
Thomas Peacock wrote
that a poet
is a semi-barbarian
in a civilized community…
the march of his intellect
is like that of a crab, backwards.
True. The more one thinks
about it…

Please permit me to go crabwise
for a moment:
Science says that
all modern humanity
has descended from
a great ice age.
We are tempered
by cosmic forces
in a biting darkness.

Out of an icy Eden,
we have followed the animals
along an edge of melting.

How frail that voyaging trickle
must have been,
so long ago
before the sun
was in our fist.

The blood remembers.
Many of us
still make pilgrimages
to icebergs.

II

But enough of our glacial past…
Our fires are warm now.
Our walls are cosy.
We are family.

The best I can wish you
is the joy I feel sometimes
in our landscape:

The sun's warm blessing
on veins
of pitcher plant.

The bell tones
of wild geese
stitching
autumn sky.
Days of soft mist
on a windowpane,
ice just a glim
on the horizon,
and a warm voice saying
come in now
and have a cup of tea.

REMEMBERING LEONARD

with Suzanne
travelling blind
we were
the river

PILGRIM

larksong
a scent of honeysuckle
on an offshore wind

my boatman
leaving
must wonder

island to myself
a tilting splatter
of forget-me-nots

morning-glories
more glorious
in sea light

   once years ago
   from this beach
   in a breaker's curve
   I saw
   a garden

PATH'S END

abandoned orchard
ghost nets
across November

hard to believe
this bush
once burned
in wasp song

as if enchantment
could make
a house
appear again

suddenly a stranger
I crawl out
of the thicket
on bleeding hands

sad beauty
still sleeping
and guarded
by greengage limbs

SANTA FE TRAIL (2013)

prayer flag
leaf on cobweb
in desert wind

far from home
fierce New Mexican sun
and I the only one
foolish enough to be out
with my father's shadow

over late afternoon
sand dunes
seven crows
and a story
yet untold

recalling home
moonrise
knocking Mars
from apple tree

again sad steps
O moon
rising
to piss
in a foreign land

NORTH LIGHT

abandoned cove
    finding myself
    among the missing here

in a rock crevice
sea wind finds
the violet

crows above long grass
Van Gogh
without cornfield

chin music—
my dead grandfather
splitting wood

my father's last boat—
a moon rocking
in bilge water

wild cherry
summers
on the tongue

thoughts
of not being
here
when flowers
split the rock

VIKING SITE

northern El Greco
L'Anse aux Meadows
in fog-loom

damp grass
distortions
the sod house shifting
into the great hall

wind down from Greenland
lost souls ride
loon's wail
into landwash

what beast
moving in the mist
has carved itself
from a spar
of driftwood?

TO WILLIAM CARLOS WILLIAMS

so much depended
upon them
they thought

academics
attending
your early readings

determined
to fix
your wheelbarrow

uneasy
with things
as ideas

anything free range
like chickens
rainwater

and poetry

TWELFTH NIGHT

Twelfth Night, a sad time,
before we knew Shakespeare's night,
Jim and I, mummering

in gas mask and tin hat
found in his uncle's cellar
under drifting snow.

Twelfth Night, an end time,
soon to our separate schools,
the tinselled tree cast out.

Twelfth Night, mysteries,
rumours of ghosts, and an old man
pointing out the "she-moon."

Gas mask and helmet,
lit up by her brightness
in the bitter air.

And later, in the last house
that night, a woman crying
as we ate our cake.

Twelfth Night long ago
and Jim and I left wondering
why the woman cried.

THE GROVE

the grove
where they kissed
grows circular
in memory

motes dance
shards of sunlight
prick the meadow

crab limbs
grab at them
going under

a swish of leaves
the gleam
of tossing apples

winds dally
dragonflies
stitch the stillness

my first teacher
and her boyfriend
shadows
in the aftergrass

GOD'S DOG

Old Man Coyote
knows the way
we've chosen
isn't the way.
Any name we give him
isn't the name.

Long before we came
into his territory,
Native Americans knew him
as God's Dog.

Old Man Coyote,
bounty on his head,
someone we have
to exterminate—
trap, shoot, poison,
kill in whatever which way.
But still his numbers grow.
World without end.

Old Man Coyote,
creature of opposites,
clown, creator, destroyer,
alpha-omega original,
always the lesson for us
to lighten up,
get serious,
pay attention.

II

Lover, magician, trickster,
supreme shape-shifter.
I hear him laughing
far off on the horizon
into which all
of my cowboy heroes
have faded.

Old Man Coyote
dipped his tail one night
into a moon pool
and swished the stars
into place,
a great sperm stream
across the sky.

If God owns a dog
that goes bump in the night
through our garbage pails,
what's the point
of phoning Animal Control?

Besides, even if we could,
where's the wisdom
in snuffing out
the scrawny old fellow
who invented sex
way back
in the first place?

OTTERS ON ALL SOULS' DAY

Otters in a pool,
five of them, on All Souls' Day,
snowflakes on the wind.

Once in a lifetime
for me, the gift not looked for,
the curtain parted.

Flames fathom far down
where some of us joined them once,
the old man of myth,
the young queen not returning.

To think that
on this day in history,
our medieval ancestors,
men in black coats
and long faces,
went calling for prayers
through the towns,
ringing mournful bells
for poor souls
in purgatory.

Otters on All Souls' Day,
five in a soulful frolic
making water foam.

LOON

We knew the loon's four calls:
a muted whoop across lake mist,
a lament unsettling the night,
a yodel of males defending territory,
a madman's laughter
somewhere on the wing.

But we listened for calls
within calls.
Lost souls, we said,
of woodsmen
who never returned from places
where brooks flowed the other way.
Our elders revelled
in a rending of the air.
Fallen angels, they claimed,
Lucifer himself, leader of the flock.
Yarns whispered of a devil bird.
Only a silver bullet
could bring him down.

This morning, years later,
alone in the woods,
casting line across water,

I catch a mad laughter
way up in the fog.
Suddenly I'm crazy myself,
surprised how my soul
yearns to rejoice,
yodel for its own territory,
laugh back

for day breaking
on a radiant river,
a world of stippled silver
all to myself.

SEARCHING FOR ANCESTORS

I call out
silently
to a stranger
who appears briefly
in a page or so
of a Hardy novel.
He's just back from
the Newfoundland fishery
and one of the most
minor characters
in the plot.

West Country cemetery
    a Hardy rain
    erasing
    names.

2009

WHERE GENESIS BEGINS

for Norma and Gail

ALL TO OURSELVES

Just the two of us,
each with a rusty can,
catching pricklies in rock pools,
culling treasures
along a grey shore.

Where is she now?
It seems so long ago,
that spell,
before school walls.

Just the two of us,
five or six years old,
landwash buddies,
fierce little stick figures
scravelling over kelpy stones,
miles of beach
all to ourselves.
We thought we'd be
there forever.

Summers fuse,
flowing to the one
time a ling came in,
strange fish
that got us arguing:
was it cod becoming eel
or eel becoming cod?
And the day of the dog
bones washed up,
wondrous
in sea wrack.

From its eye sockets
she picked shells
and moon pebbles
for luck.

When the billfish came
we believed
anything was possible.
Next summer, she said,
they'll come back
as birds.
And the hard case
of a devil's purse
dark on a rock
between us, belonged
she claimed,
to a mermaid.

Birds called beyond calling,
sang beyond song.
Caplin shrivelled, rotted,
curled into knots
above tide-line.
Dead squid shone,
became "old soldiers"
under the silver sun.

On the verge,
all to ourselves,
small phantoms
as a fog drifts in,
we squat with our plunder,
haggling, cajoling,
cautiously trading.
Rain starts to patter.

I stand, move off a bit,
fade up the beach
to pee into my can.
I fumble with buttons
and the north wind
sprays me.

Across the damp, briny distance,
I hear her laughing still,
the voice bargaining:

"If you show me yours,
I'll show you mine."

BESS

On goat-tramped hills
outside walled towns
in ancient times,
you might have been
the one cast out
to carry plague away.

Further north,
in remote hamlets,
you might have been
village whore, bog-maiden,
noose around neck,
riding rough tumbrel
into oblivion.

In the New World
of Puritans,
you might have been
a scarlet woman
tempting church elders,
labelled by scripture
for prison, stock or scaffold.

For me,
you are a recurring memory
of a trip
to old St. John's.

In a scent of grapes and gasoline
my uncle's loaded drunk,
staggering along.
I'm six years old,

stumbling to keep up,
your raucous voice
calling out to him
through snow squalls
in from the Narrows.

"Sam…Sam…
Ya knows
what I wants now…
me skin."

Suddenly, as you swing from an alley,
he's snarling, cursing,
punching you to the ground.
You crumble like a reefer.

He starts to run
and I run after him,
crying, afraid to look behind.
Pain pricks my ribs.
The wind scrapes
like a splitting-knife.
Drifting snow blurs everything.

So many years ago now,
I still hear him
laughing
on the way home
when I ask
who took your skin away,

poor outport exile,
beaten street-beater,
lady of the flies.

All those winters gone.
A child's question
still jigging in my mind.

THOREAU

FOR ENOS WATTS

I thought of you today
in that hush
after a woodpecker
somewhere across the swamp
had stopped drumming
leaving woods and fields
no longer what they were.

You who claimed
that all sound
even our speech
is the beginning
of pregnant silence.
You listening to the rhythm
of your own drummer
long after the flicker
had flown.

You in the ticking
of your mother's clock
carved wooden grandfather
behind her in the hall
when as a child
she used to get out of bed
after midnight
secretly
sitting on a summer doorstep
savouring the world's silences
and growing up
in the lilt of warm evenings
falling in love

with quietude
along Concord's Virginia Road
when lowing of distant cattle
carried brooks and meadows
and landscapes altered
in the strains of Joe Merriam
local farmer
not as familiar anymore
whistling to his horses
in the dark.

Years later in your cabin
on Walden Pond
you listening
to a faint steam whistle
becoming bumblebee
inside a flower
and an unknown flute player
far off in the dusk
expanding the remoteness
of the universe
another Krishna
piping the planet
into place again.

You always receptive
to the world's harp strings
right where you were.
Your pulse in time
with beetle tick
and cricket chant.

Your wakeful local night
more meaningful
than any long journey.

DARWIN

When Charlie Darwin went to sea
A silver spoon stirred up his tea,
When he returned to his own kind
A sinful thought stirred up his mind.

At least that's what some clergy said,
Their souls awash in mortal dread,
Fearing measures Charlie took
Might contradict the King James Book.

But Charlie harboured no ill wiles,
His voyage was not gauged in miles,
His new research and all it brought
Persuaded him to shun the cloth.

Most clerics labelled him a fool,
A fearsome foe of Sunday School,
So agnostic and erratic,
Disturbing what the Lord made static.

Vicars bivered, grim and pale,
Got hung up on a monkey's tail.
Too bad such people never know
The point of God's prehensile toe.

ELSEWHERE: A POEM TO EMILY

Somebody wise once said
if you had not existed,
we would have to invent you.

Perhaps you have not.
Perhaps we have to.

I retreat again into dreamscape,
follow dark soul-maps
down secret paths
to the old parsonage
and you, wrapped in a shawl,
still writing.

Am I the body moving
between you and candle
when wick sputters
momentarily, and flame spurts back?

Am I eligible somehow
to be counted
in the old superstition
of the stranger coming?

Elsewhere, as always,
you never look up.
The answer to my question
left for another day.

Another day. Another setting.
And you, in overcast,
escaping the company
of young men in the parlour.

The kitchen, your garrison,
your tall frame leaning
over loaves of bread.
Moved by the demiurge,
you laugh defiantly.
Scorning parish superstition,
you toss crumbs on the fire
to feed the devil.

Along the moors, signs
of an ice-age,
hints of the great chill
inching back,
and you chasing your dogs
across a furze-brushed sky.

In barren, wide spaces,
face raised to parting clouds,
you wave your arms,
you call out gleefully
as a crow sails by.
Mist billows
low on bracken.
Far off, fractured
by the wind,
a curlew's cry.

Back down in the world
of parishioners,
"caught by the cold"
is what they understand,
whispering about you,
the pale one,
out one last time

to feed the dogs,
the December wind
almost carrying you away.

Alone on your last day
you sit, grooming yourself,
waiting in firelight.
The comb rattling
to the floor,
you not bothering
to pick it up.

Elsewhere. The stranger coming,
and you, most unlikely
Rapunzel,
letting
your
dark
locks
down.

COFFIN MAKER

"Sixteen inches across—
narrowest coffin
I ever made."
He's talking about Emily again,
the Brontë girl,
the odd one
from the moorland parsonage.
According to parishioners
who scrutinized her
from close pews,
she would sometimes sit
through Sunday services,
back turned to pulpit.

"Sixteen inches across," he mumbles,
knee-deep in shavings
in the damp shed,
raising his hands
to gauge the width—
as if the confines
of a varnished box
any more than those
of village custom,
could hold her.

"No hips at all,
narrowest coffin
I ever made..."
His hands wave
at window glass
to framed moorscape:

bracken-light,
leaning erratics,
lichen patches,
one inch of growth
for every thousand years,
a nib of birds
distant
on grey sky.

"Sixteen inches across."
He stresses the space,
hands apart
as if talking about
a trout
he once hooked,

the one
that got away.

GNOSTIC

When morning breaks,
These tombstones say,
The shadows all
Will flee away:
Words of comfort
For those who trust
In some bright place
Beyond the dust.

I stand and dream,
Imagine one
Long deep in clay
Without the sun,
Who while he lived
Saw ample token

That morning had
Already broken.

CAT POEM

I have no argument at all
That God sees every sparrow's fall,
But much more pertinent than that,
I wonder if he sees my cat:

Does he stare down with frowns and tuts
When she rips out the starling's guts?
From far omnipotent repose,
Does he spy rat's blood on her nose?

From many mansions in his house,
Does he lament the shredded mouse?
Does he suffer sore travail
When she leaves just the squirrel's tail?

With scarlet plumes and tufts of sable,
My step's a sacrificial table.
Does he condone idolatry
When she brings offerings to me?

MY CAT IN NOAH'S ARK

In a porthole orb of light
My cat curls in a ball,
Against the bulky elephant
She seems so very small.

Against the mighty behemoth
She's just a micro speck,
But she's been prowling all night long
Above and below deck.

There's blood stain on the planking
And feathers in the poop.
No nightingale is singing.
The parrot's flown the coop.

The mice and pigeons in the loft
Have strangely disappeared,
And Noah has been telling God
It's much worse than he feared.

But God stays silent in the dark,
He loves his hide-and-seek,
He revels in the cat-and-mouse,
His methods are oblique.

My cat's uncoiled now from her nap,
She bounds up to a shelf,
Becomes domestic as a jug,
Epitome of self.

With Noah to his knees in chaff,
Cleaning out the scupper,
Behind her placid, sphinx-like face,
She plans a late-night supper.

FROG-PRINCE

Resplendent in the ranks of mud,
Unmindful of the race of man,
I bloomed with water-lily bud,
Lolled blissful in the pools of Pan.

Cavorting in a classless ooze,
Oblivious to all amiss,
My life one lovely, swampy snooze
Before that metamorphic kiss.

Now as a prince I pace bright halls
And palace floors are prickly dry;
I plop from ornamental walls
To catch the odd bug on the sly.

Weighted down by crown my mother sits
A-counting out her kingdom's woes;
My princess screams and threatens fits:
She's found a blemish on her nose.

I keep a swamp tune in my head
Against the stress of courtly knack;
I crave the id of watershed
Caressing moonshine on my back.

MAN OF LETTERS

The mailman, buoyant, chirpy soul,
Graced morning with a matin,
And up to this point in his life,
Had little use for Latin.

"Cave Canem" said the sign,
On Professor Dictum's gate.
Lost in a translation now
Our man was tempting fate.

The beast sprang snarling from the shade
Like Cerberus from Hell,
If the mailman saw three heads,
He never got to tell.

FLEA

I know that I
Shall never see
What Blake saw
In a common flea:

Proceeding far
Beyond the most,
He even sketched
The sucker's ghost.

Poor dog just whines
And looks behind;
No need to ask
What's on his mind.

Rubbing his ass
Against a post,
He's just the poor,
Reluctant host.

THE SHOP

People always went to Ishmael's for essentials:
a cake of soap, lumpy sugar, loose tea,
hard tack, molasses from a spigot,
matches and kerosene.

His concession to luxury:
a few strands of liquorice, the odd cigarette or two.
If he was in the mood, he'd break a pack.
Warped taffy bars meshed with their wrappers,
jaw-breakers and peppermint-knobs
conglomerated in glass jars.
And each Christmas, peppered with pinpoints
and flyspit, a fathom or so
of crepe paper hung in the window
with a crumpled cardboard excuse
for Santa Claus.

Garrulous patriarchs of the winter stovepipe,
Ishmael and his cronies lounged there,
presiding on barrels and boxes,
under a snarl of jiggers and bultow line.
Nodding, winking, nudging each other,
watching what women and children bought,
a cranky, gossipy chorus
sneering through pipe smoke
at all they deemed wasteful, soft
or womanly.

Today, back home,
I find it hard to imagine any shop
was here, years ago,

on this paved postage stamp
of playground.
In dreamspace
I see the old crabby crew,
scattering,
scrambling over the toppled stove,
jumping, clawing frantically
at ghostly rigging
as the lights go out.

No survivors.
They never had a chance,
never knew what hit them,
that rogue wave
of asphalt
crashing
down.

RIGGS

Riggs always waited for the Lord's Day
to bother people,
sauntering from house to house,
asking to use the telephone.
Eventually, after warnings
from the welfare officer,
nobody would let him
make a call back home
to the outport that always
hung up on him anyway.

But Riggs still waited for Sunday.
For this, he tolerated the pills of Monday,
slumbering it all into Tuesday
when a bus packed him and the others
off to a rec-center
for darts and shuffleboard.
He snaked and laddered
through Wednesday and Thursday,
bingo cards blurring
into months on a calendar.

On Friday, when the aroma
of fish-sticks floated up corridors,
he became more familiar.
Sometimes the old mariner in him
rose up to corner a guest,
recounting once more
years ago at the ice
when the captain called him aside
to say, "You're a good man, Riggs."

Saturday night, alone in his cubicle,
stripped for a bath,
he watched his torso in a mirror,
contours of the bumpy shoulder
shaped in childhood by a blow
from his father's pitch-fork.
And the old man
glaring back at him
from Man-O-War Gulch,
that place in the north
where men sometimes went ashore
for bare-fisted boxing matches
to settle disputes
over fishing berths.

Riggs longed for Sunday.
Against whatever waited
he had the Lord's Day
and a number
scrawled on cigarette paper
deep in his pocket.

SALMON

Once in a mind-over-matter spell,
lost epoch of prime communion,
she was always mystical,
wise prophetic creature,
proficient ring-bearer,
eternal battler,
emblem of folk heroes,
patron saints and kings,
her flesh forbidden
to all those outside
sovereign estate.

This morning in low, rusty water
she is tallied
by federal government officials
at a river mouth,
entered in a book
as the first fish
for the month of August
and let in through a gate.

Tonight, in a shrinking tributary,
under alders
and cold stars,
she will gasp
in the arms
of a poacher's son.

AFTER THE STORM

after the storm
a drop
of sea foam
swinging
in the bluebell

through dark rampike
snipe call
carrying
the pond

letting out his cat
the old hermit
lets in
the moon

TEA ROOM

A simple abode. Utensils few,
plain, unassuming.
Nothing extra in the room
but a bunch of flowers,
a picture on the wall.
Even a bit of poverty.
A singing kettle,
the distant sound of water falling,
wind blowing.

My mother's place
out on the headland
almost qualifies.
She's still there at eighty-odd,
tranquil, reverent, solitary,
telling me over again,
still crafting
that story about the time
her uncle had tea
with a poor fisherman in Toslow,
the best he ever tasted—
from an old tin can.

The two of us,
over steaming cups,
philosophers
at a plain table.

In my mother's house
are many
mansions.

COWBOYS

He was a few years older than the rest of us
but that never stopped Frank, the Catholic boy,
from joining us sometimes for a game of cowboys.
How easy those days of white cloud
when granite beach became prairie,
and dry kelp rolled by
like tumbleweed.

On his last day with us,
he arrived with half a muzzleloader
and the eye sockets of a gas mask
from an abandoned cellar.
He lit us a small fire, outlaw style,
in the ribs of a caplin-skiff.

That was the day the priest came
and took him away,
without a word.
We knew little then
what it meant
to have a girl
in trouble
on the Cape Shore.

Just like that,
the Lone Ranger was unmasked,
dragged up through a cabbage patch
by a frail, sickly fellow
in a black frock.

And nobody,
not even Hopalong Cassidy,
Red Ryder or the Cisco Kid
could do a thing
about it.

No way at all
for any good cowboy
to go.

HANSEL AND GRETHEL
(A FOOTNOTE)

I am the child of the original story,
the unvarnished, oral version,
the yarn unravelled
by lamp-ridden forest wives.
I am more accident
than gift from God.
But call me Hansel too,
child of a heavy burden.
Cold darkness owns my cot.
My sister is still
under a cabbage stump.
The night is late.
The walls are damp and thin.

The woman railing in the next room
is my flesh and blood.
She and my father, teenagers,
are cursing, fighting,
out of money again.
Sometimes a wind draws nails
above rowdy talk
of sealers in St. John's,
Yanks in Argentia.
He's drunk, as usual,
back from quitting his job
on the military base.

I am the fearful child,
forever framed
in the savage tale
before any editing
for culture's sake.
Small comfort to me
that in future texts
a scapemother
will be dragged in
to die
for our sins.

CHILD ON MICHAELMAS

dusty parlour
        saints above
        canvas
        cold to the feet

window horizon
small cloud
becoming
        wing

frost-clipped
        aftergrass
devil in blackberries
watching bull
        mount cow

knife on grindstone
        armoured angel
        more frightening
        than any
            of his fallen
            kin

goose
      feather
on the wind
      glimpse
        of petticoat

leaf spatter
late
butterfly
asters
shimmering in ditch

ASTERS

With summer gone
and you in the fall of something,
suddenly turn one day,
look over your shoulder,
and there they are,
stars in the ditch.

You whose ancestors,
before any chaos
of Michaelmas,
once knew a goddess
who cried
petals of patience
and afterthought
down to a parched world.

In stardust you were young once,
in love, on a shaman's path
to divination,
your quest for charms
and panacea
coming on.

Today, in another September,
alone on a back road,
you glimpse purple markers,
galaxies underfoot,
reminders
that no explosion,
this side of the first big blast,
could better the silent one,

when these petalled asteroids
        and all
                their relatives
collided with
receptive earth.

SALTBOX HOUSE

Saltbox house,
surreal in the shimmer
of a summer day.
Cluster of tourists stepping
gingerly over the black dog
asleep on the doorstep
into a world
of chiming clocks
in caskets ticktocking
against each other.

> Pitchfork in bucket of cast-net balls.
> Faded Coaker posters. Door-prize tickets.
> Cod oil bottles glinting
> blue on window sills.
> Postcards for sale.

Adrift in sun motes,
(no boats in the bay)
the tourists come and go.

> Curled tidal charts,
> calendars, sheet music, stacks
> of newspapers. Studies in sepia.
> A Bible weighed down
> by a cannon ball
> dug from turnip clay.

> Lace handkerchiefs, letters
> from overseas. War ribbons
> under glass. Wedding dress
> on rickety table
> beneath shotgun rack.

Ebb and flow of voices.
Easy talk layered
like varnish. Somebody telling it
like it was.

Flatirons, teapots, cold kettles
anchored on cast-iron dampers, and

aproned for the occasion,
knitting on straight-backed chairs
in the back kitchen,
three old women,
watchers from a Conrad novel.

Outport museum.

SOLOMAN KANE

Solomon Kane,
beloved principal of the old school,
was an outport legend.

Sometimes in a rage,
he'd leave the room,
race over to the merchant's shop,
dip his strap
into the pickle barrel.

Solomon Kane, master
of the bloody switch,
respected for pounding
Euclid, arithmetic
and the Laws of Moses
into students' heads.

Today his last homily
towers up through nettles
on a tombstone
in an abandoned churchyard.
"The dead in Christ
shall rise first."

He waits deep down
in glacial clay,
pinned by prongs
of juniper roots,

still teaching.

LOT'S WIFE

Flat character. Cutout
illustration for a Sunday school lesson:
                    disobedient woman.
We never even knew
her name.

But flesh her out, remembering
all flesh harks back
                    to fire,
imagine reasons
for her looking back. Grant her
at least curiosity.

Some say two married daughters remained
in the holocaust.
But the story leaves room
                              for options:
What about other relatives
and friends? What about enemies?
Was she bored with God and religion?
Indifferent? Stuck in a rut? Sick of her lot?
Perverse? Tired of taking orders from patriarchs?
Did she have lovers
burning for her in Sodom?
Did somebody in the smoke
                              call out her name?

Irit, like the child in the fairy tale,
stooping furtively,
pocketing bright pebbles
                    for the way back.

Big bang over her shoulder. Irit
swerving, staring back into genesis.

Irit, woman as landscape.
Salt of the earth.

Alone on the barrens,
by a solitary leaning rock,
I sometimes hear her name
chirping
in my head.

NERO

Don’t dwell on Nero’s bloody rule,
Ignore the persecution hype—
Aside from fleshy weaknesses,
He was a pure artistic type:

Philosopher, fine poet too,
Actor, musician, wit;
Crowned by brilliant laurel-wreaths,
Each a perfect fit.

Forget he butchered wives and friends
And locked dull plebs in fetters—
Pedestrians were out of place
In his world of arts and letters.

Don’t go along with dullards,
Discussing his mortal sin;
Don’t say he fiddled while Rome burned—
He performed on the violin.

Don’t be a blatant philistine,
Don’t be a picky vulture;
Denigrating Nero
Is denigrating culture.

CALIGULA'S HORSE

Caligula, wise man of course,
Sought due promotion for his horse:
With no prerequisite debate,
The beast became a magistrate.

And then one day, without a groom,
He clopped into the Senate Room,
Followed beastly intuition,
Became an instant politician.

Without regard for poll or slate,
He soon demolished all debate.
And senators called out for more
When he did wonders on the floor.

With misdemeanour as the rule
He was a true unbridled fool,
Guided by a brute suspicion,
Stamping out all opposition.

He was reviled by common folk,
Democracy was deemed a joke;
To quote the ancient anecdotes,
He once said, "Let them all eat oats!"

Now that he's passed beyond declension
His legacy deserves attention;
Some politicians to this day
Still emulate the equine way:

They clop and neigh, they snort and roar,
There's always something on the floor;
They pound their desks, they're downright corny
Making all the issues thorny.

Don't wonder when they clown around
And seem so shockingly unsound;
Just trace the madness to its source:
Caligula adored his horse.

HOBO BILL

God's secret service is inscrutable.
His spies are everywhere,
an eccentric, wandering cast
of characters.

Hobo Bill called himself
a student of the night sky.
I saw him one time
staring upward,
radiant in a teeming rain,
smiling like the beggar
who once disturbed St. Augustine,
though Bill was no beggar,
not even your typical hobo.
He just answered to the word.

Dressed year round
in dirty parka and galoshes,
he looked like a blend
of bearded prophet, philosopher
and mountain man,
expecting nuclear winter
to happen any day.

Snowflakes were flying
the last time I saw him
labouring east on Water Street,
swinging two mop handles
for walking sticks.

In the last cold spring of his life
he was evicted
from the apartment
where he loved to read books
by candlelight.
Forced back to the streets,
he slept on a park bench
near City Hall.
When civic authorities
removed the bench,
he was left
to sleep on the ground.

Hobo Bill,
on his back
in the dark again,
gazing at galaxies.

The night sky
was what he wanted, so
they made damn sure
he got it.

PAGES

In scattered folios
of autumn whispering
I listen for your walking
somewhere behind me
in a night now out of print.

I know I'll not look back
from this stillness
listening in first frost
in the hushed scriptorium
of emptiness.

I'll keep on walking
along the sidewalk symmetry
of November sheets
as a back-yard breeze
carries paper scraps
across the night.

XANTIPPE

They said Xantippe was a shrew,
But what else could the woman do?
Her husband was completely free
To teach young males philosophy.
And most amazing to the masses,
He took no money for his classes.

So she was left, with child, to spin
And worry when the bills came in.
While he sought meaningful debate,
She grumbled to an empty plate;
While he defined the common good,
She combed the hills for firewood.

His robes were torn, his eyes looked odd,
He bore a message from a god;
While people joked at her demise,
Some oracle declared him wise.
They etched his likeness on a frieze:

There by himself,
Was Socrates.

HERMIT

Tonight, while politicians
in a town hall meeting
are proposing extra taxes,
forcing him
to develop his marsh,
something is pumping,
in the swamp.

On his last couple of acres—
oong-ka-choonk.
The old stake-driving,
solitary drummer is back.

In an explosion
of suburbia,
he listens for the boom
of the bittern.

NEW YEAR'S MORNING, 2000

FOR GOLDA WATTS

The world stayed
with us last night.
No aliens danced
on pinpoints in space.
No angels opened books.
No Christ led armies.
The Second Coming
postponed again.
No comets seen.

Just snowflakes this morning,
driven on the wind.
Frost webs, flowers
in window corners.
And, blown off course,
by the last storm
of the millennium,
one small bull bird
tangled in a thorn bush.

Cradling it carefully
in a towel,
we took it back
down the beach road
to find its grooves
again
on the biting wind.

And, on the way back,
stumbling toward us,
as if a scarecrow
had slipped from its cross,
a man in ragged pyjamas
trying to flee
from a nursing home.
Some poor fellow,
not quite making it,
captured,
wrapped in a blanket
by white-coated people
in a van.

SLIPS

"Slips" he always called them,
moving away from us
in woodsy October sunshine,
rabbit snares coiled
and bulging in his pockets.

This is years ago.
Mother is spreading a picnic blanket.
I cry after Father,
but Mother comforts me,
explaining he won't be long.
Waiting, I toss chuckley pears
into a swift brook,
watching them
swirl away.

He returns in a scent of turf,
squashberries and pipe tobacco,
sitting on a blanket
to tell me things:
I learn that rabbits
turn white for winter,
their feet are lucky,
and a brace is two.

Now, many years later,
just the two of us
in his hospital room
on a snowy afternoon,
he in his final dementia,
a Lear of sorts, babbling
in his own
great storm,

and I, crying inside,
wanting to follow him
again.

"A great place for slips," he says,
indicating the white walls
and the long, fluorescent corridor.
"Rabbit paths all over the place."

"Do the doctors catch any?"
I ask, playing along, and
just for a second or two,
the old hunter arrogance surfaces,
the planter's entrenched resentment
of all authority:

"They wouldn't catch shit,"
he snarls.

THE LAST KEEPER

He has kept a light,
but not the proud, familiar one.
The lanes are safe now.

Not like in the day of
those men looking down from frames
on the cold, grey wall.

They had their shipwrecks,
storied rescues and storms;
they were sometimes heroes.

He has kept a light,
the great silver arc rotating
through dutiful days;

careful records too:
caplin-scull counts, bird-calls
low in evening light,

and sketches of shells,
watercolours, sea-carved
landscapes abounding.

Now, in his last week,
as decreed by Ottawa,
he has seen a sign:

a trout ring appearing
at last in the small pool
he stocked three years ago.

Just for a moment, today
by his pruned rose-bush,
he feels the ancestors

looking down on him.
He straightens up suddenly,
peers off to sea.

He has kept a light. Ottawa
and the ancestors both
can go to hell.

THE SECOND WIFE

Mornings alone, abstracted,
at her window by the sink,
she would watch
the boat's wake
widening, disappearing
out the bay.

She often secretly wished
for north-easters
to keep him ashore,
but they never bothered her much,
she said,
his solitary trips back home
to the abandoned island.

Last night, however,
just before bed,
everything changed:
He was trying to tell her
how hard it was
for an aging man,
crawling on his hands and knees
into the brush,
to bring a graveyard back.

Suddenly he was a stranger,
a crazed pilgrim
to a past she hardly knew.
Who was this caretaker
of white palings
and headstones
out in the middle of nowhere?

Why could the woman in the moss
not stay buried?

That woman
who would always be
twenty-six.

THE LAST HOUSE

According to legend,
a bird fluttered
into the great hall
of feasting one night,
above all the music and chatter,
window to window—
then was gone.
And the harpist looked up, singing
our life is like that,
one brief, bright moment
between two darknesses.

This morning I am alone
on the abandoned island,
in the last house standing.
The fires are out,
the music gone.
The feasters have left the table.

I followed something
up from the landwash,
small, ruffled, grey,
flitting in through a warped
doorframe,
out another.

In from buttercups
and rat-tails
strumming
on the wind.

Out into sea light
and strings of morning glories
tuned along cellar stones.

GOAT AND APPLE TREE

The scene seems medieval now,
seasons in tapestry,
poor perspective, flat village on
hillside,
a goat forever on hind legs,
devouring the crab apple tree.

Sprightly, a fixture
on grandfather's place,
devil and doctor at the same time,
he lived with us once,
kept on by superstitions
barely stirring in the blood.

We were surprised the tree
survived, even prospered—
uncanny relationship—
tree and goat symbiotic,
as if each took the other in.

Rickety with age,
the goat collapsed one morning
on a narrow ledge
high above the sea.
The carcass hung there for days,
distant in crow space,
twisted like dry tuckamore,
before it fell.

But the gnarled tree,
the only thing standing

on the homestead, still lives.
Last year, hanging on
to a handful
of wilted fruit,
it kept a stray robin alive
well into winter.

This evening, crossing the fields,
I see a limb in ghost frost
dangling one last apple—
        old, shrivelled scrotum,
        shaking on the face
of a full moon.

FOGSCAPE

FOR STAN DRAGLAND

Loren Eiseley once said
that fog made him feel free,
unobserved,
himself,
gave foretaste
of what it means
to become ghost.
How wonderful
he might have felt
in Newfoundland.

Once, on the Cape Shore,
I heard a woman say
she found "company" in the fog,
the way things shifted
each time she looked up
to that gap in the hills
where her son walked off
one morning years ago,
on his way to the mainland.

Alone today, on a headland,
I wonder if anyone or
anything sees me
ghosting near lighthouse
and solitary grave
of the keeper's daughter,
young woman of another century,

still
in this place
where the wind ties knots
in tuckamore.

Salt on my lips,
reminding me again
of origins,
luminous abstractions
of first chaos.
Fog eradicates horizon.
Surf pounds rock.
Sea birds haggle
somewhere.

I am brushed out
in the immense flow
of a Turner landscape
where solid forms
are sacrificed,
smashed
in a sun-wobbling vortex
of silver,
strangely liberated
in my insignificance.

1993

IN HARDY COUNTRY

With love
to my mother,
Marjorie Dawe,
prime among those
who never let me forget
that best
and worst
of places,
my own hardy country

IN HARDY COUNTRY

For me, it's no county overseas,
no Avon, Berkshire, Dorset,
no Hampshire, Wiltshire, Somerset,
no ancient temples, no mounds anymore,
no West Country nappe all manicured now
for a museum trade,
no classical Max Gate drawing-room
where Florence died.

For me, it's those drawn outport figures
in Bonfire Night,
the nip of a north wind and mummers'
accordions rising on a moon…
As the fire expires
the stranger in the kitchen
is spinning a story
about one of the last criminals
to be hanged
out through a courthouse window
for a crowd on Water Street…

It's my mother too and the way
that she looked at me once,
so wistfully,
in wood-stove light,
recalling her young womanhood
in a Canadian Depression,
and the wonderful man
she was going to marry
in Montreal before any rumours of war,
or just some small coincidence,

perhaps,
in that far summer
on St. Catherine's Street,
made her return,
regretfully,
to Newfoundland.

A FAIRY TALE

My great grandmother
is a young girl
lost in the woods.
She carries a berry basket
and cries
because she has no money
to drive the fairies away.

Watching her,
I am old enough
to be her father.

Her path sinks deeper
into red turf
and bright leaves are sharp.
Old wood has reaching arms
and grey, knobby legs.
Branches are glowing fingers
that cup and cradle the sun.
Faintly, she hears music
on a soft, sap breath
and knows it is not the brook.
Far far away are calling boys
with jam stains on their lips
and laughing girls
clumsy in black, rubber boots
and a clang of dippers.

Just before twilight
she walks out of the woods
and finds a young man fencing
near a crab-apple tree.

He runs to his father
for a horse and cart
and offers her
a ride back home.

On the long way back
through lingering,
still-twig light
they sit close together.
He hums an old love song
learned by some fireside.
The grass is long and green
right up the middle of the road.
Between her knees
she holds her day's berries
like a cask of jewels.

I am patiently waiting
to be born
and wondering
when the cart
will turn into a turnip
or a big red apple on wheels.

I call out to them
as they slide down
gradually
into leafy sunset.
Waving my empty dipper
I run after them.
But they ignore me.
The night closes
around everything.
And strange stars
come out.

RIDDLE

I see them in summer
twilight,
six or seven sitting in a kitchen.
The lights are not on yet
and my father comes
in through the door
from the day's cod-splitting.
Behind him the horns of a new moon
rise up from a cloud bank.
The tide is pulsing
up the ladders of a stage head.
Cleansed by an afternoon
of blood
and salt-spilling,
father is straight and tall,
joking as he takes the beams
on his shoulders
and joins the others
in a riddle spell.

Patient as anchor rust,
he awaits his turn
before he offers:
"What goes over the water,
and under the water,
without touching the water?"
In the pause,
the sea whispers.
Then grandfather answers:
"An egg in a duck's belly."

My mother,
six weeks married,
smiles coyly
in a corner.
Much against their wishes,
she has been swimming
all by herself
again this afternoon
over on Swan Island.
She has not told anybody yet
that she is expecting me.

STILL LIFE

From the fall of the wind:
a cap full of crab apples
brought to a kitchen table
by my nine-year-old sister
from a garden
near a beach wall.

(Somewhere in pock-marked light,
my mother is weeping.
That cap, tossed from a train
one Sunday afternoon,
has reminded her again
of my brother
who is seventeen
and somewhere
on the mainland.)

By those bitter apples:
two baccalieu birds
bleeding
near a china bowl.
(Father, in a shadow
near a gun-rack,
is always returning
from another day
on the water.)

(Grandmother, old pious penguin
with her apron on,
waddles down
from her picture frame.

With a sweep of her arm,
she scatters my paper and crayons,
telling me to go
and do something useful
for a change.)

DEVIL AT THE DANCE

Somewhere in the lore of long ago
In the place where I come from,
A stranger appeared at a dance one night
As a man of music and song.

The young and old revolved in his reel,
He fiddled the stars from the sky;
The Devil assumed such a pleasing shape
As the time went spinning by.

But just on the verge of cautious dawn,
Someone spied his cloven foot,
So he disappeared in a brimstone cloud
And a drizzling rain of soot.

There's not one trace of that floor today
Where weeds grow lush and long,
But people all along the coast
Still wonder if the dance goes on.

THE BOGEY MAN

He was always
somewhere
in my bedtime dread
in the looming shadows
when mother threatened
to put the light out
if I didn't get to sleep.
Famished for child-flesh
he waited in a moth-ball cave
behind coat-hangers.
And on that first day
when mother released my hand
in the windy school yard
he assumed the form of a bully
watching me from the bridge.
Later, in the long lane
back from the store at night
when I was afraid
to look behind
he was footstep-echo
and whispering breath
on the back of my neck.
And there were places
along the coast
where he appeared
as the Black Doryman
or some questing devil
in a ghost skiff
roaming the waves
in the ungodly hours
to snatch youngsters

straying on the beach.
In talk of war time
he was a foreign sailor
spying on us from a fog
or an American from a base
coming to carry girls away.
One day we were alerted
about a strange character
near the edge of the woods.
I could see his wolfish eyes
peering from dark boughs
when my aunt warned us
that he might even be
a Canadian
or something…

SOLSTICE, OUTPORT CHILDHOOD

deep snowfall
  still
    black hole
  of tadpole pool

hands around tea-mug
  an uncle
    remembering
  winters
in the lumberwoods

grandmother
  spinning
    daydreaming
her own version
  of rumpelstiltskin

cleaned for christmas
china
  along aunt clara's dresser
    light
from the sea

UNCLE

Soap-scented, shiny by the lamp,
You looked down from your chair,
My brother's nose was dark with blood,
His knuckles bruised my ear.

You'd give the winner fifty cents,
You swore aloud by heaven;
My stocky brother was almost eight
And I was a skinny seven.

In a kitchen with the fire out,
We fought a savage round;
Father and Mother were gone that night
On a Saturday trip to town.

Outside, a devilish wind drove by
And rattled from eaves to floor;
We knocked some dishes from the shelf;
Your rum breath called for more.

You laughed and said we fought like men;
Your frolic cast a gleam;
You clutched that silver in your fist
The night you turned fifteen.

PEPPERMINT ROCK

If somebody asked me
for my earliest memory,
it would have to be
that day in Avalon
when I, just a drooling toddler,
dropped a great peppermint knob
into my infant brother's mouth.
There in the crib cage,
below a framed picture
of somebody's guardian angel,
he was kicking and crying,
a gaping hole of a mouth,
one chasm of grief
through which my world
was tumbling.
To appease the spirit
of this pit,
I rolled one of my precious
candy boulders
to the brink of the lip
and let it slip…

Here everything goes mad:
the baby, blue-black
swirls upside down
and mother
is slapping his back.
She is shouting at me.
I scurry under a table,
her wrath like a dogfish
after me.

I wait for that worst
which always happens.
Up in the glassy pictures
the ancestors all frown down.
Queen Victoria grows
another layer on her chin.
The guardian angel goes
for his or her sword…
The candy,
a slimy shiny ball,
chuckles on the floor…

I can laugh at it now,
the way I tried
to stuff his face that day.
It is only in my moralizing
moments
or bouts of self-pity
that I want to change this poem
and call it my earliest lesson:
how a gesture of pure
unadulterated generosity
can be so misunderstood,
or an act of kindness
can sometimes kill.

ONE FALL NIGHT

Back in that forever
of growing-up to touch the sky,
back in those after-supper times,
there were long fall nights
when a full moon seemed to pull
on the stalks of the fields
and the old grey picket-fences
keeping all within bounds.
And there were a few big houses
stretching stories into a sky
that we could never reach.
One night we crept away
from those houses on the skyline,
from their frames of kitchen light
across a light frost marsh
down to the river that ignored
all lines of field and fence
as it let in the rising tide.
And big silver sea trout came in
on the pull of the new moon.
We heard them splashing
in the water below the fences
where we sat quietly,
so high on the top rails,
on the skyline now
with the houses we had left.

OUTPORT CHRISTMAS

Once a year, at least
my mind becomes lined
with yellow paper
from old attic trunks
where sea-gulls glide
in a scent of apples;
cold turkeys recline
on china slabs
in delicious death
as I carry yet
the weight
of a pregnant woollen sock.
I stare through frost glass
holding up a cross;
I watch strange humps of rock
on the eastern snow.
The sock gives birth:
exotic candies
little shepherds
plastic fishes
on an icy morning floor.
I stand
holding the empty skin
under the darkness
of a dead tree
nailed to the roof
yesterday.

ON SMALL ISLAND

on path moss
    up from landwash
leaf sounds

in from sea
    cat paws
through long grass

bisecting pool
    and sky
the muskrat's wake

raindrops
    rock reflections
in lily pads

from grass spear
    sun drops
into pitcher plant

BOATMAN

I was taking my time,
sculling her back
from her husband's funeral
on that abandoned island
where he had asked
to be buried
with his ancestors.
She sat in the prow,
stiff as a figurehead,
watching the others
row on ahead.
Being just a boy
of twelve or so,
and free from school that day,
I thought her ancient
as the Old Hag of Nightmare,
but, looking back on it now,
she might have been
thirty or so,
all sad and lovely
in September sunshine.
With time on my side,
as I thought then,
I coasted,
letting the others leave us.
She never said a word,
even when I stopped
to watch mackerel spray
westward up the bay,
and sea trout swirl
near a river mouth.

Soon, all around us,
the sea was looking glass,
our cove a bowl of silver.
But when we reached shore,
she spoiled it all
when I heard her say
to a man on the wharf:
"What I'd like now
is a nice bit of salt fish."
And all I could think about
was her own poor man
alone forever
on that island
where loons bawled
in the evening time.

I thought she was callous,
cold, indifferent then,
but perhaps I was
much too literal-minded that day,
hardly the boatman
for the journey
she was taking.

CARETAKER

I've heard it all before
from this wizened fellow
who comes each summer to tidy up
the old Methodist cemetery.
Today, an aged Tom Sawyer
without the apple,
with time on his hands,
he wants to regale me
with talk about the good old days.
He's fondling those markers again,
re-tracing the lettering,
stroking lambs, handshakes, harps
and cold angels carved on the tops.
He's stressing the warning
in every epitaph,
a fateful anecdote for each:

Once again the grim plight
of Poor Isaac
falling on his gun
in far beaver-country,
and young Richard cutting his foot
long before any miracle drugs
were around to save him;
and the legend of Oliver Brown
struck down by lightning,
and poor infant Sally,
forty years or so dead
from strawberries out of season,
resting there with her mother
who was nineteen herself

when she died.
He steps gingerly over a family
all victims of Spanish Flu
and whooping cough…

Soon he will switch the subject
to nuclear war,
the Bible
and the Middle East.
I wrestle with a weed-locked gate.
Any second now,
he'll be in ecstasy again
proclaiming no peace for our time,
pronouncing
that the world has come
a long way
from the safe
and steady place
it used to be.

A DAY IN '45

I lived as a child then
part property of girl-aunts
and grandparents
in old parlour pictures
that moved
in growing up
in sticks of grass
around large thickly painted doors.
Somebody talked of "mushroom clouds"
and I looked up into a cloudless sky.
There was a hanging smell of gun-powder
around old muzzle-loaders
but only in a dusk-dark hall
of boots and coats.
And there were long cartridges
in back-room boxes with rabbit snares
and powder-horns and fishing poles.
Down beyond the house
my puddle was calm, mirror clean.
Not a ripple stirred the lily-pads
on a day when a rock was dropped
from the sun
into a distant sea.

THE DEAD BOY
(CIRCA 1946)

Coppers on his eyes,
A new king's head right and left,
And sisters crying.

Coppers on his eyes
And grandmothers telling us
Of clear, golden streets.

Coppers on his eyes
And someone lifting us up
To see their shining.

Coppers on his eyes,
Enough for two candy canes,
But shop blinds are down.

SUMMERPLACE

aspen
          pane-tapping
tap dance
     in the dark

     rain roar
the peak of my grandfather's roof
     parting
               the sky

in lightning
               flash
                  ancestors
          sepia
               frowns

ABANDONED OUTPORT

Sun on boarded windows
and gull cries
high in August clouds.

On a small beach-path:
blue-bells nodding
over driftwood.

A bee is buzzing
inside dark cracks
in a window pane.

Clover meadow:
above the rusting ploughshare
a butterfly.

A sudden fog
and sea-winds
bend the sting-nettle.

Deep in graveyard grass
snails and lichens
cling to the headstone.

Across the schoolhouse floor:
paper scraps, dry sea-weed
and a dead moth.

Against the cold twilight:
dark picket-fences
and a crow's flight.

In a rising moon:
a church steeple
and lilac leaves.

AT WESTERN ARM

There was once a saw-mill here
giving a swift brook
its last fling
before it found the sea again.
There were houses too
with small front gardens
where lilacs shook
in fiord winds
and somebody turned earth
to plant an apple
or a rose tree
or some spot
of bleeding hearts.
Between the gardens
there were snaking
narrow lanes
where sweating horses toiled
between the mist of dawn
and lantern light.

Now everything is gone
down
in a tangle
of alders
and the slow
revenge
of the birch.

DARK MORNING

A phantom ship drifts by
The yawning cove;
Cold kettles are anchored
On cast-iron stoves;

Damp dories bob
In metal north-eastern light;
The beach holds perished caplin
Of last night.

There's not one upstairs scuff
Of woollen sock;
A short hand points to four
On a rusty clock.

THE MUMMER

I was once the best mummer
in our cove.
I pleased the people
all the time.
And through the Christmas spell
I mummered by myself
across drifted fields
and tricky paths
above the cliffs
on raw nights
when sea voices whispered
in caves far below me.
I clutched my kerosene lantern
and felt my old accordion
wheeze against my ribs.
And in all those winter times
with my light coming to hers,
she always let me in,
though she never guessed me
and I did not lift my veil.
Not once did she guess
that all those tunes I played
of long-gone summer love
and never-forgetting
were just for her.
Though they danced and laughed
and shook the china on the shelves,
her youngsters could never know
how I played for mother alone.
Though they shone
with cake crumbs and syrup

on their happy faces,
I never played for them
in that salt-box house
where stove pipes cracked
and stars winked
on the snow outside.
And that big, lazy man she married…
least of all I played for him
snoring on the settle
in the chimney corner,
a red face so peaceful
with the tea-pot waiting
and long rubbers limp and steaming
by the blushing stove.
And in all those years
of forget-me-not tunes,
she never guessed me
and my veil stayed down.

THE OLD MAN AND THE MOON

We laughed at him then,
that old man so intent
on cleaning herring
with his finger nails.
We laughed at him
with silver scales over dirty fingers.
And we laughed
when he commented on the news:
"God'll never let them reach the moon."
We were boys remembering
back just a couple of catches
when we saw him smoke in silence,
watching his swaying nets drying
across the face of a rising moon.
He believed he saw a face
in the shine up there.
And we laughed then
as he talked to himself.

Now we are scattered men
remembering
back along a fish-spine row of years
to that time on the coast
of his belief
when the moving herring-schools
mooned in the long night tides
and tangled in the waiting nets
just yards below his quiet house
where he slept.

FIGURES FROM ANCESTRAL LANDSCAPE

wind in the beams
grandmother's hands
kneading bread

mackerel offshore
south wind shadows
in the after-grass

tap-dancer at wedding
turning to watch
his shadow
on the wall

leaving the house
of the newborn
midwife
under winter moon

pause
in old husband's tale
the fool's laugh
and the March wind

THE BEAR

Once in a long-gone time
before any people came
and the island's trees
were spears of ice
against the frosty stars,
it came ashore
and used the land
as a stepping-stone
in polar-ice infinity.
The great tracks
in a wandering, crypic chain
from shore to shore
were there for days and nights
before the snowfall
filled them in.
And dark spruce resounded
as rising surf
rolled ice offshore.

Years later, when a few people
lived here, there was once
a long winter famine
and the fish all gone,
and a grave-digger toiling
to get through frozen earth.
One day in this starvation spell
it came back again,
walking out of a white blizzard
like some clumsy giant
from the children's books,
walking towards the village guns,
bringing the famine to an end.

In another age, when only the old
remembered the hungry times,
it came ashore one day
from loose ice-pans
unlocking from the shoreline.
The people watched it cross the beach
on its way past flakes and stages
and low root-cellars.
With spears and guns
they tracked it to the tree-line.
Later, in a seaport town,
they charged admission, ten cents
to look at the carcass
propped up with ropes
against the wall of a merchant's shed.

Years later, with the island abandoned,
two boys returned one spring
to fish for trout
in the land of their ancestors,
and on a night
with pebbles clattering in landwash,
it returned, staggering,
brushing by their tent
on its way down river.
Next morning they found the body,
stiff under fly-buzzing
on the warm beach stones,
the head all swollen
where it had starved so long,
a tin can stuck
on the gangrene tongue.

Tonight, in a glow from television,
descendants of the island people
half listen to somebody
reading the late-night news,
reporting yet another
roaming near a town dump,
and government officials
on their way with the proper drug
to put it asleep,
cart it away somewhere
from civilized community.

COMMUNION

In a faint memory of '52,
I can see the elders still
quaint like Gauguin's Breton folk,
or sometimes
creating the hell
of an old medieval masterpiece
where devils feed endlessly
on human flesh.
I can hear them too, arguing
and laughing on windy nights
in an aroma of cod
and kerosene,
when it was told
how the Devil
could take the form
of a great loon
laughing at us poor mortals
from somewhere
in the misty tide.
I can see a kitchen
and shadows crossing
on wallpaper.
The men are just back
from gunning
and, steaming on a supper table,
the carcass of a big loon
on a platter.

EVENING, BARENEED, CONCEPTION BAY

A cold wind
creeps unmarked
through an old picket fence
and eats the salt-stained grass
already dead
on a skull of rock
above the bay
spilling itself
on the teeth
of kelp-ringed crags.

No birds in flight
on a slab of sky.
Beyond
across a bight
a slow mist hangs
in a cross
in a block of window light.

THE WATCHER

Once in Hemlock Cove
when a war
was somewhere
overseas
one man
was told
to check the lamps
each night.
And in the shadows
he walked
whistling to himself
secure in making sure
no German planes
far up in the mists
would ever know
a community waited.
But one night
he watched a young woman
dressing by a kerosene glow.
He watched
at her window
not bothering to tell her
of the "douting rules".
A half-naked woman
not worrying
about the news
from overseas
watched
by a man
who told himself
just this once
that one small light
would never matter.

THE NAKED MAN

In a wet August day
with salt wind on berry leaves,
he loomed in fog
across a cape
and bog meadows slanting
down to an ocean's roar.
Around him dim cattle stood
still as rock piles
in the driftwood light.
Above him gulls screamed
down the dark tide
and gannets darted
in the herring shine.

I asked him to come
to guide me
down through the marshes
where the pond was hidden.
But he had fences to mend
and cattle to tend
and a sure way for me
to find the pond myself.
His face was granite smiling
and offering a chair
by a cracking stove,
and a brown china mug
where kitchen saints

smiled down
through kettle steam.

Later, in half-gone morning,
I found his marker
to the pond,
his naked man
of piled weathered stones
and snarls
of dead juniper stump,
precarious
and leaning
on the tundra
wind.

Still later, returning
timidly in twilight,
I crept by the rock man
silently watching me now
wandering back
to my road-sign world
with small trout counted
in a plastic creel,
watching me
slipping on pathless moss,
grouping
in metamorphic shadows,
in bog-sucking footsteps
away from those cryptic stones,
me, the most naked man of all.

THE WIDOW AND THE BUTCHER BOY

"Paddy's comin' in a sleigh,"
She met him at the door,
A little house in a stony field
Engulfed by the ocean's roar.

A fisherman's widow in Torbay,
Behind her a fire bright,
And he a small boy with sausage to sell,
Afraid of the wild March night.

"Paddy's comin' in a sleigh,"
She smiled at his puzzled pause;
He wondered what her Paddy could do
Three months after Santa Claus.

She spoke of her sons, all overseas,
A row of dim frames on a wall,
A place with the saints all staring down,
Astir in a flickering pall.

"Paddy's comin' in a sleigh,"
She warned that he must be good;
Her round face shone in the warm spruce light
As she bent for a junk of wood.

She paid him from a coin purse
That hung like an old wet sock;
A fistful of buttons and candy
She drew from a fractured crock.

"Paddy's comin' in a sleigh,"
She chimed as he left the yard;
He chewed on a piece of peppermint
And swallowed very hard.

"Paddy's comin' in a sleigh,"
She echoed awhile in his head,
But he was too young and Protestant
To cherish what she said.

PEGGY

They laughed at this simple girl,
she who was not like the others.
She who could be promised the stars
would let the boys do anything
for a coke and cigarette.
She shocked everybody
with her wild talk
of trees shedding blood
and devil's mark on haddock skin
and what she herself had heard
the animals say
in their dark stalls
on Christmas Eve,
and her visions of fairies
by an old wooden bridge
when the moon floated
on the tops of water stalks.
They made fun of the way
she scrawled pictures
of animals with wings,
and how she wept sometimes
at the clicking
of her aunt's knitting-needles
evenings when the sea called.

Finally the day came
when everybody left the cove
for good

and Peggy died
in a city somewhere.
But as the years passed,
those who had once laughed at her
began to talk
of going back
to a cove of bliss
with bobbing skiffs
in blessed light
and quaint little houses
with good wives knitting.

Now there was a new way of believing
what ancestors had believed,
and a roundabout return
to elemental matters.
There was talk of exiled poets
scattered over cities and towns,
waiting out their lyric lives
for a chance to go back there
one more time.

MARSH

sun on whorl
    of pitcher plant
    and finger tip

scattered raindrops
    your fistful of berries
    pattering on tin

    mist on my face
white light
through wing of dragonfly

    heat ripples
moth dance
over beaver sticks

VORTEX

Back home now
on that island
a window pane is broken
through which an ocean sighs
in a grey room
in a seeping dawn
and shadows
of wet sashes
and veins of glass
are netted
on an eastern wall.

I am there now
because I am away
from that room.

In a washed-granite stillness
in a spell of pebble light
a salt wind freshens again
and tunes departure's ode
through all sharp edges
of that window
and my vortex.

Perhaps a true homecoming
is really
a going-away.

CAPE SHORE WOMAN

I

(Before the Birds)

Waking before dawn,
Alone there in a big bed,
She waits for bird song.

In a north window:
Grey sky and dwarf spruce leaning
Back from sea strain.

Christ like a split cod
Across wallpaper shadows
And clock ticking.

Old things in her head:
Legend of the robin's breast
And ocean's roar.

II

(Getting Wood)

Going up the beach
Against the wind,
Gathering driftwood,
She stops
Suddenly
Still
Seeing
How close
The sandpiper
Will come.

III

(Shell Spell)

Sand spray
Stings
From the south west.
Turning
To make sure
She is alone
On the beach,
She tilts a shell
Against her ear,
Listening
For another sea.

IV

(A Tune)

Through kitchen window:
Dark notes
Of seabird
On silver sky
Turn white
Across cliffs
And sea caves.

From caverns
Behind her eyes:
The flutter
Of an old tune.
Tapping her foot
She tries
To coax it back.

V

(She Remembers)

When we were youngsters
back on the island,
I used to be mad after Joe Manning,
a fine strapping fellow
who could row a boat all day.
Once, at a dance out in Patrick's Cove,
I stood around all night
but he never even glanced my way.
God, it was tormenting
watching those wonderful arms
swing Kitty McGrath and Rosie O'Keefe
right off their feet.
Then, somewhere
between the jigs and the reels,
he left for Canada
before the war broke out
and he never came back
til 1982.

Life's a dance too,
I suppose…Ah, yes…
At a wedding in Placentia last year,
in loud music and the youngsters' fun,
he fumbled his way
across the hall
to dance with me.
He the pale scarecrow now
with the hair white
and face caved in,
and spindly arms
coaxing me off

from the wall
and my vision
of shoulder muscles
shiny and pulsing
like a stallion's
and wind-browned arms
and a ripple of oars
across a swell.

VI

(Trucks)

As fog creeps in
And spruce fade on the hills,
She stops to rest
Her water-bucket down
And watch four trucks
Pass up the winding road,
More antique dealers
From another town:

Dragged through the mist,
A motley mound of chairs,
Dark tables, trawl-tubs, clocks,
One gypsy chain,
Strange licence plates,
Ontario, Quebec,
The same to her,
One dusty, slipshod train.

Tonight she'll dream, perhaps,
She's young again
Out selling tubs
Of berries in the town;

Or, back from death,
Her husband baits a trawl
And curses on
The cold rain coming down.
Four sons fade away,
No time for fuss,
They're leaving for the mainland
On a bus.

VII

(Fireplace)

Tom Power's old place:
And the only thing standing,
A pile of flat stones.

Rocks from an island:
Chimney in the long grass swell.
Island now once more.

Fires in her head.
She strolls in sunset.
Sea breeze fans the land.

Warm foundation stones
Where the ghost stories came
When the nights were long

And Mary's kettle
Whistling against the frosty times,
Dancing on the grate.

STAGE

No putt putt of the motor boat,
no waiting women placing boughs,
no children playing in the cliffs,
no cod-oil doors with painted moons,
no meadows green through caplin,
no sound-bone talk from tired men…

But one grey fish-stage
leaning seaward
from cold sloping rocks
below the meadows
of the unmown hay…

TOP OF THE WORLD

Found this afternoon
at a flea-market:
an old rectangular map
called Top of the World,
just like the one we used
in rough, unready school days,
something free
from a mainland candy factory,
one big-as-life chocolate bar
adorning each corner.
And we in our frosty
hardtack times
were right up there,
bold print declaring it:
the big island of Newfoundland
in top of the world form.
But one day
in the bottom of winter,
a tattered group of us
were punished
for drawing our own
dragons of sorts,
a series of smutty pictures
across the wide, blank spaces
of open sea.
In spirit, we were not
so different really
from old, cautious cartographers
who sketched in sea monsters
as stays against emptiness,
or our methodical ancestors,

who were always in a hobble
about charting their ghosts,
those comforting spirits
so necessary in barren spots
between communities.

A CONSECRATION

Luke remembered
their last days on the island
gathering what was
to be taken
as young gulls swayed
above the sun-grazed swell
and a lingering mist
ghosted in the garden gleam.
And he remembered
the clergyman telling them
to burn all the boards
from the dismantled church
because such wood was consecrated.
But next day Luke's brother came
in a big white skiff
and took the wood away
to build a house.
And as the months passed
Luke was uneasy
about the anointed wood
until the morning
when he heard the meek cry
of his brother's firstborn
within the sanctuary
of the new walls
as dawn stroked window glass
and kettle mist ascended
to the sturdy beams.

IN A SMALL COVE

Sheer cliffs in sea-song
And seeking in close spring fog,
Sheep above roof tops.

THE FRENCH SHORE MAN

Seems I can mind them
myself,
the French
along our coast,
and poor father
and his father before him
talking about the wonderful bread
those foreigners made
in beach-rock ovens
in the summertime.
That was well back
in the rowdy days
when they thought
this shore
belonged to them.
Sometimes they seemed pretty human
all the same,
giving you one
of their queer loaves
to go with your fish
when you crossed paths
on the water,
even though you were English
with wife and youngsters
on the shore.
It must have been hard
for them to accept defeat
and leave the coves
where they cured their cod.

I remember
poor grandfather grinning,
claiming he broke bread
with them one time
somewhere off the Grey Islands…

On raw days now
when the wind is in
and the sand taps
my window pane,
I can close my eyes
and see them
moving
in the landwash still…
Dreamy foolishness, I suppose,
for me with sixty summers notched.

But one day
six years ago,
I was digging a hole
to put the bark-pot on,
when all of a sudden,
my pick struck Frenchmen's bones.
Seems there were two of them
laid out there.
One had no teeth at all;
that devil yawned at everything.
The other had all his ivory,
no mistake about that,
and when I laid his skull
on a rock,
he seemed to stare
out over the water,
grinning at it all.

BONFIRE NIGHT

Quick stray snowflakes
and a squall
up from Baccalieu
through the dogberry trees.

The shouts
of youngsters.
A doll
on a long dark stick
swings
against the night.

On billows
of collapsing
cod-oil drums
the bottomless dory
lifts
  one
    last
      time.

THE BALLAD OF FLORA

The widow, Flora Livingstone,
Was lonely in her bed,
With lots of money put away,
Poor husband Sam was dead.

A strapping lad named Billy King
Who kept her cattle fed,
Was lusting for her seaside fields
With voices in his head:

"You're thirty now, she's sixty-odd;
She's picked you as the one;
Present her with a wedding-ring,
She wants a man, my son!"

They married in the month of May,
The fog released the sun,
And a fiddler from far away
Led off the village fun.

Young Billy King was gloating now,
He'd put up with her bed,
He owned the cattle on the hills,
He saw good times ahead.

The warm wind darted in the hay,
A summer's silver thread;
In lobster-crawl and snipe-bawl time,
A worm stirred in his head:

"She'll grow more feeble with the fall,
Her time cannot be long;
You'll still be spry when she is dead,
Your limbs are young and strong.

But Flora flourished with the years,
While Billy's hair turned grey;
The sea wind darted to his bones
When fog rolled on the bay.

Something of fey in Flora's face,
An old man in her bed
A-snoring in the snipe-bawl time;
A worm stirred in her head:

"He'll grow more feeble with the fall,
His time cannot be long;
You'll still be spry when he is dead;
Your roots run deep and strong!"

IN PICASSO'S "MADMAN"

Somehow, in Picasso's "Madman,"
I can see the four of them:

Uncle Henry Gaunt
just back from the Labrador,
bent over Aunt Carrie's grave,
crying in his big, cupped hands,
then stopping suddenly
to peer through knotty fingers
at aspen leaves
trembling on a white sky.

And my tired grandfather,
daydreaming in the landwash,
gazing through a web of caplin mesh
strung on his splayed fingers
in a moment
when he did not see me
watching him.

And poor Jenny Drake,
the war-bride
knitting by a kitchen window,
ignoring her baby's crying,
staring through the yarn-lines
in her thin fingers,
talking again of cowslip fields
and heather-slopes
across the sea.

And the retarded boy
who lived one time in Rampike Arm,
lying hidden under cherry-limbs,
talking to his contorted hands,
laughing excitedly
to himself
each time mosquitoes clustered
for his blood…

…Something of four people
I knew one time,
now glimmering
in Picasso's tattered "Madman"
forever fascinated
with those invisible skeins
all tangled
in his scrawny hands.

HAIKU (1)

dawn flecks
in lees
of buttercup

doryman
lifts herring-net
and morning moon

HAIKU (2)

sunlight on the wing
seagull ascending
over chapel ruins

somewhere
from white cloud
a cry of tickle-ace

HAIKU (3)

cliff-top tuckamore
goat hooves ringing
on a shale sky

mushroom cloud
man against sky
with hay on his back

HAIKU (4)

after northeaster
    spreading seaweed
on her flower bed

on rain-washed wall
    the shadow of a pitch-fork
        and afternoon sun

HAIKU (5)

lying in alders
waiting for loon's cry
to take shape

water strider
stirring clockwise
on the moon

ON CUSLETT BROOK (1979)

Just the three of us fishing there
in the purl of an August afternoon:

On my left, upstream,
through leaf filigree,
caught in a glint
of mote-dancing sunlight,
my young son
so Icarian in summer energy,
spin-casting metal
into pools of sky.

On my right, downstream,
my father,
eternal worm-and-bobber man,
stirring from a partial Buddha stance,
bear-like in beach rock haze,
shambling around
the last pool
before the sea.

I dream Silver Doctor
and siren tug
on double-tapered line.
I have the middle water
all to myself
and a line or two
of old Heraclitus
in my head:
something about our never being
able to ascend the same brook twice.

EDWARDIANS (OLD PHOTOGRAPH)

For them it is always Sunday afternoon:
six couples in the shade of a tree,
lounging in an English meadow.

They are blurred now:
sepia smokers in straw hats
lolling among wine bottles,
cake-baskets, clover.

They stare out at us:
lotus creatures, insolent somehow
in languid pose,
smug, sprawling, laid-back,
locked there in weekend.

Behind them, over daisy-dotted trench,
a jacket swings carelessly
on a strand of wire
dividing the property,

winding, coiling towards the Channel
perhaps, one inconspicuous,
barbed, metallic cord,
not really symbolic
in this landscape yet.

BACK ROAD

As I walk by the house tonight
I am wondering
about Walt, Fred, Tom,
Doug, Steve, and Sam.
They have disappeared somewhere
on the mainland,
have not been back home
since they left in the sixties
one by one.
I wonder also about Geraldine
who was glad that summer
to cross the gulf
and live with an aunt
in Cape Breton for good,
and young Madaline
who perished
on the streets of Vancouver.

I find myself recalling
how short childhood was
in a past with not much
time for play.
I see them always
in hand-me-downs,
tending rocky meadows
and damp potato drills,
and cod to be cured
from rough water
four miles away,
the curse of the puritan
pervading everything.

The parents are alone tonight,
keeping the big two-story house
as best they can.
Samuel is seventy,
Nora is sixty-nine.
The lawn is tidy
with their own toys now:
Creatures from the comic strips
crouch everywhere.
Samuel just polished
a plywood Garfield yesterday.
Last week he removed the moons,
painting circus ponies
on barn and cellar doors.
And Nora, this Halloween,
kept one grinning lantern
lit up in a window
all night.

THE VETERAN (1)

I'll not forget that foreign scene,
And I just a frightened boy:
He tarried there in my rifle-sight,
So tall on the clearing sky.

I struggled to pull the trigger then,
For, just beyond his head,
Was a flash of something close to home,
Across those fields of the dead:

A wink of sea between two hills,
A gull's turn on the sky,
I stopped and put my rifle down
And let my man pass by.

THE VETERAN (2)

"Take what you can
From those you kill,"
Our commander let us know;
"A watch, a chain, or anything,
Whatever you can stow."

I didn't heed him at the time,
I didn't want their gold,
But one day on a gory field
When wind was whipping cold,
I snatched a locket from the neck
Of a German boy I'd shot;
He was sprawled face down
In a muddy pool
And blood was spilling hot.
The locket had a golden heart
With two smiling women inside;
One had to be his mother,
The other one, his bride.

And there in cold rain
And the raven's croak,
I flung that keepsake away,
A locket like the one I wore
For Mary and Mother that day.

WILD GEESE

They are passing by, low again,
as they did five summers ago,
their wing beat stirring
the yellow afternoon
of sky and clear pond waters
back through pliant mounds of turf
warm above wave-lilt
over mossy stones.

This was always
my own fishing place
until one day five summers ago
I met him there,
a bent man berry-picking
who said he always thought
this was his secret pond,
but never mind…
I could have it now
as his legs were not
what they used to be.
We sat eating berries
where the brook departed,
watching two wild geese
rise slowly from the lily pads,
their shadows grazing us
as they turned westward
to fade over distant rampikes.

Today I am watching
the two great birds again
rise up as if a bell
were sounding somewhere

in the partridge berry hills.
They swing westward
where sky meets marsh leaves,
their shadows almost
touching me.

SANDPIPER

It hopped
across the pool-streaked sand
as the tide was coming in,
with legs like straws
that would not bend,
and a low, piping call
on the rising wind.

It skipped
along the mussel-beds
as the sun dropped
from the sky,
and faded somewhere
in the surf
with a lonely, twittering cry.

IF SONNETS WERE IN FASHION

If sonnets were in fashion,
I think I would try one
about a dog I heard
barking one time
in a taped poetry reading
by Robert Frost.
The imagery would be geological
and the old man of fire and ice,
plain diction, the gravel voice
could have the octave
all to himself,
free to be crafty
yet seeming so undesigning
within the confines
of iambic walls,
his presentation glacial, powerful,
moving on the slow import
of its melting...
And then, intruding into line eight,
in a tree-at-my-window pause,
that audible fossil,
just for a couple of seconds,
a dog barking faintly somewhere.

The creature would have the sestet
all to himself,
so perfectly autonomous out there
in pussy-willow swamp
and prime New England sunshine,
casually scanning its territory,
cocking its leg

against the world perhaps,
its primitive spondee
lingering and wonderful.
Oblivious to any
iamb or anapest,
it would just be
its own wild poetry,
a summons
from the wordless places
once again.

"STRUGGLE INTO LIGHT": A POEM TO JOHN CLARE

"A struggle into light,"
was what you called it,
your flash into a fame of sorts
in a world
where rustic bards like yourself
were going out of fashion.
Yours was a sun-on-a-petal spell,
a dart of robin-red,
quick trout-dapple
in the dawn.

I can picture you too
glowing for awhile
in old London town,
stomping big country boots
along cobblestones,
a bit of a Bobby Burns
in your homespun jacket,
your love of ale,
and twinkle for the lasses.

When you arrived back home,
trying to find poems
in the fields again,
there were curious souls
always coming by in carriages
to see what a peasant poet,
so unlettered and all,
could be doing
in his element.

It must have been weary, John,
with fields to be tilled
and babies to be fed.
One time you called it
"wearing into sunshine"
when those literary folk
dropped by and called you
from your labours.
And you complained too
how you were promised books
and all kinds of patronage
before they dropped their heads
in smug, "Good morning attitudes."

Years later, in your final fading,
did you expect very much
when they shipped your corpse home
from Northampton Asylum in 1864?
Could you believe that nobody,
not even one of your own,
would come to receive you?
Could you ever see
your remains
being waked in the shadows
of a village pub?

And, as for your last request,
when you asked for burial
on the north side
of the churchyard,
right in middle ground,
where sun could linger
on your grave,

did you expect
that they would grant you
middle ground?

Were you surprised, John,
when they moved you south
to the coldest side
where the sun hardly lingers
at all?
Were you somehow
expecting it
when they set you down
in cold clay
where the shadow
of a chancel
falls?

ALDERS

Last night I dreamed
they were bringing the world
back,
verdant tongues calling out
to a sun again;
but we were no longer
a part of it.
There had been great snows,
grey rock, and serrated forms
against a sky.
Millions of what we used to
call years had passed
before that
spear of green
between two stones,
that thrust of arrowhead.
Always apprehensive
of their coming,
we had massacred
in the name of clearing,
we who had whittled
small music sometimes
from their supple bones.

Fearful of advance scout,
of any forerunner
of wilderness,
we had always killed
messengers.

METHODISTS

It is a Sabbath evening
in Edwardian Newfoundland
and the house is being readied
for my great grandfather's passing:

a few last words to a semi-circle
of souls around his bed;
the murmured consolation of Scriptures;
the adjusting of big feather pillows
around his head;
in a corner, a woman's whispering,
re-creating the strange white bird
against a window yesterday.

Outside in a dim hallway
more whispering,
a solemn shaking of heads
recalling his meticulous clearing
of the droke two days ago:
too much for one man
with axe and mattock, they said.

His wife seeks out his prayer-book,
his Orangeman's sash,
his good suit all pressed,
put away systematically
for the proper occasion.

Now only one thing remains:
somebody must go out
and knock on the door
of the Methodist church,
ask them to keep the noise down
so a man can die peacefully
just up the road.

BITCH

She appeared in the season of small leaves,
stopping to beg
outside our gate one day.
I was seven that summer in caplin time,
and she had been foraging
along the beach,
scrawny, black and white intruder,
little lone ranger
among the gulls and big crows
who watched her suspiciously.
I had been warned
to stay away from her;
dogs were useless anyway,
my father said.
Besides, she was almost blind
and flies droned around
the damp mask of her eyes.
But I still swear she saw
me clearly that day, watching her
in the slow dust of afternoon;
our communion
crossing centuries somehow,
before I tossed a crust of bread to her
and ran.

Years later I found her bones
in boggy woods beyond our cove,
no attitude of begging
in them anymore:

and up from an eye socket,
the pronged genesis
of an aspen tree.

Today, so many years later,
in a strange city,
in an arid valley
between apartment buildings,
I hear wind in an aspen tree:

that silver-green clicking of dry bones,
all those little dry bones
reassembling.

CALLING THE CHILDREN

Somewhere at a lane's end,
through nettles pinned on boggy twilight,
and the frame of a rusting car
upside down in cherry blossoms,
the children are barking
bare-footed in puddle mud.
And mothers are peeping
through metal frames of windows and doors
and calling "bedtime," "Billy,"
"Jane" and such.
The fathers who used to
swim in that almost-gone puddle,
are sleeping in front of television sets.
The children do not hear
their mothers' voices;
they have sharpened spears
from fingers of the cherry limbs
to kill all the tadpoles.
And now in the going sun
the pool is muddy blood.
They will take their own time
coming home this evening
carrying sweet blossoms
for their mothers' hair.

DAEDALUS

Alone on the beach this morning
I catch myself
blaming the gods again
for this poised gull
against the sky,
mocking me now
as they did once
at my son's funeral
when a partridge laughed
from somewhere
in the grove.
I dreamed that day back
with gentle sea swell,
goats, green island,
the lip of a grave,
and sorrow planting me
like some tree
twisted
in sea wind.

On morning wings
across the sun
he comes before me,
there at the seabird's core,
my son,
the slave-girl's child,
that shadowy
all-too-human form,
five-pointed man
inside translucent feather.
Cruel are those gods

who coax
with sunshine!

Now I am forced
to see him
falling
once more,
clawing
the air
so far
beyond
my pleading.

And as he goes
by me,
one last
glimpse
of the slave
girl
free somehow
in frightened
contours
of his face.
And the mesmerizing
space
of it all,
the small flag
of a foot
disappearing
into the shimmer
of the herring
shoals.

And far away,
as if they know
about it already,
waiting, nodding,
placed there
for my returning,
sinewy, sunburned men,
like a chorus
of cormorants,
picking their snarled nets
along a sea-wall,
voicing their platitudes
against all heedless youth;
the mesh of an old hubris
closing in again.

DAEDALUS AT GARDEN WALL

On the day when I finished this wall,
he was only five or so,
playing with clam shells
in the landwash below me.
I was anxious that morning,
fearful that he might wander off,
go following goat-paths up the cliffs,
slip away somewhere
into the kelpy murmur.
So I called him back,
kept him close, talked to him,
until the work was completed.
And then, into my last patch of cement,
while it was still wet and pliable,
I pressed his small hand.

Today I find myself stepping back
to admire the mark,
the short fingers splayed
like rays of sun
in a child's drawing.
The hand is fading now,
edges crumbling as I stroke it.

Back on that day
I was confident craftsman,
one stoical
about what the rain's chisel,
the sea-wind's hammer could do.

Today, alone in the wall's lee,
I am shocked
by the corrosive power
in a sparrow's song,
a blade of leaf,
a snail's crawl,
a shadow of scudding cloud.

SEABIRD

The oil-soaked carcass,
seaweed ganglia,
broken glass,
in a whirl of sand

Under shell crust,
that fearful something
from the tar,
the center holding.

Alone in front of it,
I daydream.
In my own crude circle,
thumb meeting index finger,
I conjure phoenix.
Matting the dark form,
I seek relief
in raised design
of cameo.

But from noon's shimmer
over fly-blown stones,
the desert's warning

that art will not be
sanctuary

this time.

HIDE AND SEEK

It was an August evening,
just after supper, in 1949,
when six of us met
for hide-and-seek
in the shadow of Uncle John's
slaughter-house,
"the shammel" we called it.
Freddy Smith lined us up
and started counting:

"Eenie, meenie, miney, mo..."

Marie was the first to go
and she with the swinging pig-tails
went wraith-like
laughing across an oat field.
On the next tally,
Skinny Charley followed her,
loping like a hound dog.
Soon Judy and panting Alice
went tumbling after.
I was left with Freddy
eager to count himself out
and call me "It."
His finger, like a lance,
tapped time on my chest
and the rhyme raced on,
one mad cacophony.

"It's not fair," I called
as he raced away
across the stubble.

I was alone
near the blood-tub.
A quarter moon
sickled on the sky.

"Eenie, meenie..."
I counted on the clapboards
waiting for them to call.
The blood of last week's lamb
came up on honeysuckle.
I waited..."miney, mo..."
but all was quiet.

And then the years passed
and I heard from Marie again.
Seems she married an American
much against her father's wishes
and when she telephoned, in 1960,
crying from somewhere down in Alabama,
the old man wouldn't
even come to the phone.
Skinny Charley bled to death
in Viet Nam,
just after he'd sent his brother
a big beer-mug
shaped from one of the shells.
In 1978, I found Judy,
cosy in a Boston accent
and vowing she would never
come home again.
Alice and Freddy crossed paths
and got married
somewhere in Ontario.

Last year, at the conclusion
of a poetry reading in Labrador,
their eldest son
came up from the back
to say how small the world was
and wish me well.

1981

ISLAND SPELL

To Whom I Owe So Much,
Jacob and Marjorie Dawe,
My Parents

GHOSTS

I remember: cow-bells waking me
and mid-wives walking
in yellow flowers after June rain
and stone doorsteps
brought somewhere up from spindrift
and crying babies with eyes closed
like drowned kittens
and old women tying silver coins
around the necks of the newborn
and waving nettles over driftwood
on our short-cut to the swimming hole
and granite under crystal tide
and going with buckets to a well
under green-gage trees
where a big trout waited to be fed
and every leaf-killing fall of the year
a loon coming to the salt pond
to be shot again
and people leaving houses for cellars
on nights when the wind blew hard
and lead jiggers hanging in haylofts
where boys and girls went hide-and-seek
and men with faith that the fish would stay
and pirates leaving graves and gold
and guardian spirits
and thin boys stumbling behind horse ploughs
in silver fog low over turnip clay
and fat men dressed for Sunday
walking ahead of their women
and young men flinging their hats
from trains to Canada

and Americans building their bases
and sick young girls leaving home for good
and flower gardens
and kitchen gardens
and lilacs in the lane dust
and pendulum clocks always swinging
at weddings and wakes
and sun and moon and tide and wind
and wallpaper leaves
and lamplight
and window-blinds
all up and down...
all ghosts.

THE FAR ISLAND

Now in late November
looking at the far island
in snow-flurry light,
one lives on faith
that flocks will dot the cliffs again
in warm, caplin-spawning,
whale-blowing,
meadow-waving,
waterfall spells.

Locked in mainland winter,
I look across the dark tickle
and the purple stone
still has its halo
of sea-birds.

THE POTATO GROUND

In April the Easter snow came
pooling between dead cabbage stumps
in her kitchen garden,
the old woman who charmed toothache
and banished big, seedy warts
from everybody's hands:
in white shopping-line
one knot
for every wart
and bury that line
in the damp potato ground.
She always warned us
not to try fishing-line
because it was slow rotting
and your warts would stay.

And in time
sore skin would heal
as sun warmed longer
and moss greened
on her western wall
as fog rose
from felt-roofs
in seed-stirring days.
But sometimes
in the fall of the year
you saw the warts all resurrected
as knots of canker
on dark potato skin:
Gnarled fingers pulled them up
and flung them off

towards another ground
out on the slate, swelling sea
where more cold fingers hurried
knotting stiff cod-lines
for the long trawls
of the winter fish.

INTERVAL

The oats lean seaward
In the weight of morning rain.
A scythe rings on stone.

ONCE BY THE ATLANTIC

There he was
with his back to the cove
and his tune to the passing crowds.
In the fishy, coal-dust evening
I was rushing
with the rest of the city
towards supper.
But as I paused
to drop money
into his tin collection-plate,
I thought I knew him
from an outport somewhere...

He had to be
the dumb, blind boy
conceived that summer
back in Rampike Arm
when his mother was raped
by a peddler passing through.
She was weeding a garden,
a young girl alone
on a perfect day
beyond words,
she said,
and the slick stranger
who was whistling a tune
she never forgot,
crossed the meadow
and caught her there
by chance
on the broad of her back;
resting in the after-grass...

Smug in my knowledge
and stepping from the crowd,
I felt a silly omnipotence
gazing down on him there
slumped on concrete
as the evening cooled.
And then
I heard that tune…
It seemed
as if those enticing strains
were squeezed from the sea,
the arched accordion
rolling like a wave
in his ruddy hands…
Suddenly every silly notion
left my head.

THE SCYTHE

They were two young lovers
in a summer of boat rides
on Sunday afternoons
along a coast
with sun on sounding cliffs
and sandpipers darting
across small, crescent coves
where surf touched clover.

They were promised
to each other
that summer
when he started the house
in a meadow by the sea
and in spells
between net hauling
and the swinging of the scythe
through rat-tail silver
his saw was singing.

One summer-ebbing afternoon
with east wind freshening
she came to the meadow
where he mowed the hay
enticing him
to put the scythe away
and he hung the blade
on the spruce post
of an unfinished wall
and arm in arm
following a path in long grass
they found his dory
and rowed away

to a far, blue island
where the sheep were grazing.
And they never returned
to their meadow again
and their unfinished walls
by the whispering sea.

The blade swung slowly
when the wind rose
and in days of patient rusting
all the posts turned grey
and the grass went wild
and leaned in on the floor.
And the sultry dog-days passed
into frosty dipper-nights
when the moon itself
was a hanging blade.

Years later
it took strangers
to complete the walls
on a morning
when nobody was noticing
a warped crescent
hanging in post shadows
when the wind was sharp.

Over the years
the house changed hands
a number of times
and often with hushed talk
of ghostly sounds
clawing in the walls
on raw, wild nights
when easterlies possessed the bay

and rain had fingernails
whenever people huddled
and whispered of spirits and such
as the wind went by
in the dark outside.

Years later
when the house was old
another young couple came
to that rat-tail silver
by the coaxing sea
and planned their cottage there.
On the day
old walls came down
the scythe was found
hanging in the musty stillness
and she came to the meadow
to laugh with him
as he flung the blade away.

Through waving hay
they wandered seaward
as gulls through white clouds
raced across the sky
and sheep clustered
in the shade of beach walls.
Two happy lovers
resting on clover mounds
and watching one small boat
tend nets offshore.
Two young lovers unaware
of that story
long before theirs
and that slow, fitful swinging
of the scythe.

WHITE HORSES

Out in sable winds,
White horses roam the dawn sea.
Beached fishermen watch.

THE GUITAR PLAYER

In that long-gone summer
everything moved around the fish
and one guitar player
who strummed the nights
down conner-lanes,
so sure of his strings
that moved us all.

We, the young,
would always follow him
to sing along
and watch his fingers
when ocean called to hayfields
and dead tom-cod pulsed in landwash,
their mouths wide open and round
like choir children's.

Men late at splitting-tables
kept listening for his songs
and remembering
courtship grasses in rose-light
fading in a flounder pace.

Young wives sent him cake and ale,
requesting Kitty Wells and Faron Young,
listening with windows up
though caplin rotted in the dandelions.

And big sisters
panted with requests from grandmothers
listening in big, four-poster beds
for the sad, sweet ballads
of the great men gone.

And we were little boys
waiting in chain around his feet,
waiting for him to teach his chords to us;
we grew impatient sometimes,
bored in his many pauses
when his hand slid up
the sweater of the nearest girl,
and everybody waiting,
listening for his chords
to ring again.

ALONG THAT COAST

It was said
that a vessel ran ashore here
one night long ago
when rain-wind whined
and rattled window panes.
And there was talk of wracking
and a false light
tied on a wandering goat
shifting somewhere in the cliffs.
And there are people living yet
who vowed they heard
the cloven hooves go by
as fires died in the stoves
and the ocean thundered.
One man told of a pausing at a door latch
on his way to salvage
and looking back
at a crucifix in lamplight.
And a woman in a chain
of grave-digging days
stared sadly into her tea-cup
and remembered all the widows
in foreign places.

Today old men pick berries
on the headland
and watch goats grazing
in the wispy pockets of the cliffs.
Today these men will tell
how their fathers slaved
dragging bodies from a winter sea.

And they will tell
of "outsiders" coming in
and giving the place "a bad name"
by shooting at government signs
that mark the spot
where the wreck occurred.
Offshore small flocks of birds
skim in the grey swell
and a long oil-tanker
glides in the blue haze
of a far horizon.

THE STRANGER

Perhaps the man in the hayfield
not far from the ocean's edge
is not quite old enough
to have been around here
when the ghost roamed
this hilly, dusty road.
Smiling, he comes toward me,
hanging his scythe on the fence
and preparing for a mug-up.
He drinks cold, milky tea
from a whiskey bottle
and says,
between mouthfuls of jammy bread,
that once a drowned, foreign sailor,
some stranger
from a passing ship,
drifted into a cove nearby.
He points across a hummock
to cliffs where tickle-ace skim
in mid-afternoon light.
Perhaps that stranger
was the ghost
who attacked a priest one night,
he says,
and warns me
that people around here
don't believe in ghosts anymore,
and strangers like myself
would be better off
not even asking…

We seem to drift apart…
but he keeps talking
with bread in his teeth
and me wondering
if he sees my drowned face
with eyes all gone
to the tom-cod's picking,
and soaked, wrinkled skin
all dropping away,
and little shells still clinging
to clothes brought up from somewhere
five fathom down.

He smiles to himself as I turn
my gaze seaward
to that quiet cove
with its glimpse of landwash
and a passing flick of sandpiper.
He has stopped talking now,
and he throws back his head,
sucking the last cold beads of tea
from his whiskey bottle.

THREE IN THE SUMMER AFTERNOON

A bee is droning
Somewhere in the oilskin sleeves
Of a tall scarecrow.

On strawberry leaves:
Shadows of scudding, white clouds,
And warm sunshine.

As the wind changes,
The scarecrow's arms flap wildly
In a scent of kelp.

ISHMAEL REMEMBERS (1)

I dreamed about Hemlock Cove
again last night
and all the dark woods
up through Uncle Bob's grove
made a long saw-blade
on the after-supper sky.
The full moon was rising,
burning cold orange
at the edge of the juniper twigs.
From the woods
came the far cry
of some animal in pain.
And I was a boy again
just back from the woods
and my rabbit-slips,
a boy in sweaty wool,
listening to old Aunt Grace
sooty-handed by her oil lamp,
telling the youngsters
of the fairy-paths
and the man-in-the-moon
with a turn of sticks
on his back.

ISHMAEL REMEMBERS (2)

I remember crowds of strangers
with cameras and suitcases,
coming to our wharf
summer after summer,
people who were always struck
by our salt-of-the-earthiness,
humility, and stuff like that.
But even as a youngster,
green as after-grass,
I couldn't go along with them.
After all, what's so humble
about a fisherman thinking
that his shot at a whale
in a moment of idleness
could cause the heavens to cleave
with claps of God-grumbling thunder
and the sea to go raging mad,
the likes of which
was never seen before?
And what's so humble
about a woman believing
that God caused springs
of pure water
to trickle from the cliffs
of all the islands
so fishermen like her husband
would never thirst
while toiling on the sea?
To my mind at least,
there was something
pretty unhumble

in the way we had
both God and the Devil
taking time
to walk with us.

THE BRIDGE

Once we had a wooden bridge
that took us across a salt pond
to the caplin scull
and a crescent of beach stones
smooth as old china
in seaside houses
where big clocks ticked
in a chime of tea-spoons.
Once this bridge took children
to the swing of the tickle-ace
and the skin of the sculpin's lip
and the evenings when dim ghosts
spun silver in the drift
and the wand-swish of fishing poles.
Once two brothers were lost
when a dory foundered
in the dawn tide
and the cove's best swimmer
broke his neck
diving from a top rail.
Sometimes people threw cats and dogs
into brin bags
and dropped them from the bridge
when the tide was going out
and cruel splinters bristled underfoot
in the hot sun
with spots of horse dung
like strange relief-maps
drying in a scent of dogfish.

One evening I was the last
to leave that bridge for home
and watch a salmon leap
in the glint of early star.
I think it was the next day
somebody decided
we didn't need a bridge.
Men came in shiny cars
and called the people
from the houses
and promises were made
and there was money talk
in the ring of supper plates.
Keen saws sang for gasoline
and blades screamed
in the turn of grindstones.
Soon we didn't have a bridge
anymore.

BEACH MOMENTS, SEPTEMBER '56

Above grey beach stones
Morning is mackerel cloud
And sun on gull's wing.

Somewhere from calm sea:
The ticking of motor boats
Through the sting-nettles.

In an ancient skiff
Rudderless in rat-tail grass,
A wasp is drifting.

Lop-swish on smooth stones
And a chorus of house-flies
In the drying kelp.

On rain-washed wall:
The shadow of a pitch-fork
And afternoon sun.

On warm western wind:
White moth, a scent of cod-oil,
And a loon's laughing.

Ring around moon-haze,
And coils of cold mackerel
Twinkle in a tub.

THE HEADLAND

Above the headland:
Vectors of misty sea-birds
Ploughing the spring wind.

Across the headland:
Steep-napped hills, children's singing,
And gaps in grey fences.

Below the headland:
A sheep carcass in landwash,
And a rising tide.

THE VETERAN (3)

My cousin wasn't overseas,
Little he knows of war;
Though he boasts of bloody battle
And conflict in fields afar.

They say the conscription-men caught him
Loafing in the bight;
They dragged him bawling and kicking
And told him he had to fight.

But before he reached Europe,
The fighting was all done;
He came back with the singing crowds
And joined in the jolly fun.

He brought back pictures in a frame,
Foreign dress for his girl,
And smutty yarns for local lads,
From other parts of the world.

Here am I, alone with my wounds,
While cousin struts and crows;
At night sharp shells disturb my sleep
And a cold sweat soaks my clothes.

LOW TIDE

On fine, wire waves
Across a mile of beach rocks,
The sun spreads stale fish.

POOR PETER

"The net of the sleeper catches fish." (Old Proverb)

I remember the last years of poor Peter,
when he lamented in springtime
that he could never rest
while somebody robbed his nets.
And there were many cursing times
when he picked plastic bottles,
dead dogs, discarded dolls,
lop-sided oil drums, lumps of kelp,
and all kinds of junk
from the swing of salmon skeins.
And one May night while he slept,
a big, shifting ice-berg
large as a church
carried all his nets away.
And one fine, summery dusk,
the sirens of the south wind
called a sleek, grey shark
long as a caplin skiff
to tangle, roll up, and die
in the waiting mesh.
Another time, some foreign vessel
passing dark-hulked in the night,
caught all his twines
and carried them away…

But sometimes though,
as he held us in the web
of his story-telling,

Peter used to laugh at it all,
recalling another time
when two hundred pieces of silver
struck his only net
one night in mid-July,
and he was lucky that the war was on
and the catch could be traded
to a navy-boat nearby
for a fine keg of molasses,
some good salt-beef
and a sack of flour.

ONCE AFTER SUNDAY

"And Abraham lifted up his eyes, and looked, and behold behind him a ram caught in a ticket by his horns; and Abraham went and took the ram, and offered him up for a burnt offering in the stead of his son." (Genesis 22:13)

Once looking for the sheep with father,
when he let me steer the old, green skiff,
we stopped in an abandoned cove
and came ashore
while thunder clouds passed,
clearing the sky behind them.
And there in a spruce grove,
while our kettle boiled
where a community used to be,
I could feel the spirit
of the slain ram
on the breath of the southwest wind,
moving again
into a sun-stabbed clearing
where old altar stones were scattered
over mounds of mossy grass.
Somewhere, deep in the thicket,
through shadows of erected sap,
a small brook chanted
over unyielding parent-rock.
Off from the fragrant land
the great goat spectre
sought the sea.

TO A POET

I don't remember much about that day…
I think I was in grade two
and you were somewhere in nine
that afternoon when the teacher made fun
at your scribbled poems
and I laughed too
because the others were laughing.
I remember the yellow dust stirring
in a shaft of sunlight
and a gull squalling
far above the peaked roof
and you crying
with your head down
in a geography book.
It was afternoon in late October
with paper Jack-O-Lanterns
grinning on the window panes
and gusts of wind up from the sea
tinkering with the door-latch.
I remember you all by yourself
taking a short-cut home
and kicking spindrift
as you tripped along the beach rocks
away from us forever…
Seems it was just the next day
they said you were somewhere overseas
in a war or a factory…
And your sister-in-law
found a box of your poems

up in the hayloft
and burned every single one.
The year was falling again
and token snowflakes
dallied in the chimney heat
and white horses flew on the bay…
There was talk of you in the draughty store-lofts
and the twirl of spinning-wheels
and your song was everywhere…
Once your name was even in the paper
and mentioned on the radio…
Later somebody said you were dead
and it was so wonderful then
the way you belonged
to all of us.

1975

HEMLOCK COVE AND AFTER

For Norma
with love

INUK

Another March day had died
in Hemlock Cove;
the benighted flakes of snow
settled softly on the granite cliffs
and transformed the deck-boards
of the quiet, waiting harbour skiffs.
One by one the village lamps were lit,
supper tables set
as each house looked in upon itself.

High above the quiet horse-shoe cove
an ancient spruce
with drooping twigs
with roots long dead
clung to the clayless stone.
Overhead a large form circled,
a great bird of the dusk,
battering the increasing snowflakes,
a white spirit of the north,
a great white owl,
a stranger to this coastal region.
He swung in a great arc
near the leaning top of the long dead tree
and tried to land on a branch,
but the brittle form snapped
and refused to bear his weight;
he clawed at the air
and raised great feathers
into the heavens again.

There fell a hush on the land
with only the sounds of the night

eating up the minutes
and the quiet murmur of water on the beach.

But another stranger came that night,
a giant form in furs and skin,
a man leaving Titan footprints in the night
as he walked toward the Cove,
deeply sniffing the off-shore wind.
At intervals along the narrow road
he sniffed the oil of frying herring
from the steamy supper kitchens,
the cooked potatoes in their skins,
the hot, strong tea and rendered fat-back;
but he walked on
unseen by human eyes.
He saw his goal ahead
covered in the snow
the old deserted house
at the end of the village lane.

In some oil-lamp glow
at the back of his arctic mind
some figures moved;
giants in the fans of northern lights,
the Tunnit fleeing from his people
long, long, ago
walking away from their native haunts
fleeing in fear as he was doing now.
Long, distant Asian eyes kindled fires
on the plains of his awareness,
and stooped figures drove small boats
across a hostile strait;
they paddled in the face of sunsets,
and drove dogs in long dawns

slow in blooming;
others hurried over frozen barrens
like tiny mites in the palm
of a great and distant god.

And then, one awful figure in his mind,
a man of mighty medicine,
a man pointing a bony finger
at the frigid infinity of the horizon
and telling him to leave
and not return.

He walked with sharper images:
the feather folk who called him "Eskimo,"
or "eater of raw flesh,"
tormented his many dreams;
and the men who spit fire
with iron rods and heavy boots
killed many of his kind;
and he preferred to be the distant one,
but most of all,
he came from the Inuit,
he was Inuk,
a person,
a man.

So Inuk settled in remote Hemlock Cove,
but his home would never be there.
The Cove was cold toward strangers
and Inuk had come
in the night,
a face of dark skin
from a distant land of ice.
He had taken the shack

"that nobody owned"
and besides,
"why had he come?"

As time passed on
young folk in catalogue clothes
laughed at his primitive dress
and closely watched him
to see if he ate raw flesh
like candy as they were told.
The cold spring thawed by
and he existed and fished alone
in a graceful craft
he had fashioned from hide.

The Christian wives liked to talk
of his black "heathen" ways
and spent days and days on such fare:
"Those idols he carves in his hut,
are terrible pagan shapes,
dark, shiny, and cruel,
images of Satan!
And look at his figures in wood,
a mockery of the blessed Cross!"

"I hear they change wives,
those Eskimos."
"He probably ate his own."
"He stays by himself
for some dark purpose,
you may be sure!"

Uncle John Shane or "Deacon John"
droned on in the village store:

"He talks of snakes, and frogs, and things;
I spoke to him the other day,
fine gentle fellow
seemed anxious to speak
but he's not educated
you know;
strange he should talk of such things,
since we all know
frogs and snakes will not live
in a land if ice and snow."

"I think it's time
that more of us
made a fuss
about those strange fairy stories
he's telling our young."

And the people talked on
in the present
not noticing the rings in the wood they burned,
or the shape of plants
in the coal by their kitchen stoves.

Summer soon gave birth to chilling fall;
Inuk carried more salmon than other men;
he fared well on his own,
but they blamed him for meddling
and stealing everything
a boy or man could take:
salmon, lobster, ropes and even dwarf crab apples.

One day a group of boys bounced rocks at him,
and his stone face called them "little puppies"
as he thought of a story his people had told,

of the Eskimo maid who married a dog
and gave birth to the white race of man.
They yelled and barked at him,
as he hunched his shoulders
and walked away.

One snow-speckled night in early winter
several young misdirected drunks
beat Inuk savagely
and left him lying in the snow.
He had been walking shackward
with a codfish hanging in his hand.

The story spread, next day
that he was dead, but
next morning all they found
was a frozen cod
and blood on the sunny snow;
not even tracks or traces
of Inuk.

Nobody saw that night
a great white owl
swoop over the sleeping village
not pausing at all near
the old gnarled spruce
on the top of the hill
and darkening what moon there was
and people who could not give second glances
even when awake
to skies at night, and trees, and birds,
slept on toward another day.

STRANGER AT HEMLOCK COVE

Listen to the whisper of the night-wind,
and return with me
on its largo voice
to that soon-to-be-forgotten coast;
return on the sigh of the night-breeze
that makes men remember;
return to that age
before the people left;
return to that night
when the teacher came
to Hemlock Cove.

A late September nocturne
crept on early-frost feet
along old, wind-cleaned, picket lanes,
across salty, grey shafts of reflected stage-props
and hanging, purple blades of shale,
knifing the moonlight geometry
of undulating, quiet,
waiting skiffs,
and solid planes of white, clapboarded houses.
Two fishermen worked overtime
in washing down
as the village lamps went out.
Suddenly one of them saw it
and told the other,
a shimmering light in the east,
out in the night of the bay,
the orange-winking light
of a long, coastal steamer,
a light spilling through the distance

of black-blue sheen.
The fishermen knew that the teacher had come
so they launched a dory
to bring him in.

They were not expecting a boy that night,
but a boy he was
to those two leather men
who stank of fresh blood and salty steel;
a boy who told them his name was Sid,
with one old worn suitcase
tucked under his arm,
shivering on the moving blades of the night air,
crouched in the slimy, undulating stern.
A soft young voice
in a tone of some old regret
spoke to those craggy silhouettes
on the polished infinity
of the clear night sky,
a lofty, cold pyre
fanned by great Northern Lights.
In wonder, awe, and nagging respect,
the three merely "passed the time of night"
as the stained dory moved toward the beach
and the pebbled shadow in the cove's half-light.

Sid peered ahead to the oily shadows
of a wharf
on and off in the spiked red light
on a granite black hulk of the point
straining out
from the sleeping recesses
of Hemlock Cove.

Once on land
Sid stood with the Somnus soul
of seaman's legs,
at the end of a winding, narrow lane,
into the night of a coastline.
He peered once, then again
at the silent, large, two-storied frame,
his "boarding house"
at the top of a steep, rocky hill.
His young nose caught the basic scent
of slaughtered fish and watered soil
from a fisherman's finger
that pointed him silently on.

The lonely boy would never know
the slumbering souls
in those houses hugging the coast,
those houses cemented in a moonlight matrix
and jagged, cold crags
and clinging shrub sticks;
each structure to itself
and the whole of the night;
the rain-stained cottage of old Grace Blake
a quaint, mossy frame
held up by "strange winds,"
house of the solitary, local, "witch,"
she who had whined the prophecy
that a "teacher would come"
to Hemlock Cove.
Sid walked past the homes
of the schoolless ones,
the old and the young

in horn and ivory dreams;
children slumbering free as spindrift
in connor days,
and weaving flowers of sea-gulls,
eternities of summer suns
and polished-grey driftwood;
children who worried not
that "last year's teacher" never came,
and this same sharp September
was well-spent.
And worn clocks ticked on
by iron-posted beds
above cold kitchens in the dark,
and strong men slept senseless
towards tomorrow's catches,
as the tired, young feet of the teacher
trod softly up the road.

Old Emily who lived alone
scratched a match to let Sid in,
"one of the best cooks in the cove"
she soon fed her "boarder" and talked with him.
The young man seemed mute,
but she still droned on.
Some local breeze creaked an ancient plank somewhere…
and the moon was combed by slow-moving clouds;
he chewed his meal, gazing through the panes
trimmed with white lace-cloth
like shreds of new shrouds.
And her voice droned on into the night:
her husband was once "a schoolboard man,"
now a skeleton beneath Sand Hill:
last year her sister's son "was lost"
in a bitter March night of cruel spring frost:

the schoolhouse was poor, repairs were "dear,"
they "needed a master for over a year;"
whole sagas she spun
of the fates of the few
"who taught in the Cove;"
the "lovely maid who had to leave,"
the clever parson who taught
"and was drove"...
and on and on towards the dawn
when she would show Sid a room
in the gloom at the top of the stairs.
From this night on leaves of September,
the month blew by
as babblings of winds in distant shells:

the puckered, brown face of old Grace Blake
somewhere above a half-remembered morning gate,
refusing to accept "a boy"
and insisting that her prophecy
would yet come true;
and young, scrubbed, expectant faces
melting now in a background of September sky;
a scent of melting crayons and crushed lead;
the bigger boys in hip-rubbers
who scorned
the "new ways to do sums,"
and young girls' faces smiling
out of the flowers on catalogue dresses;
dead leaves from the hinterland
drifting by rattling windows
and children inside "getting through their books;"
the tapping of October rains
into the lead spirit of November days,
and the first "repair quarrels"

with prim Deacon Shane as the head of "the board;"
the knocking of cracked, draughty doors
in the razor lips of early winter winds,
making a little class move closer each day
in a circle around the big, pot-bellied stove;
blue fingers wrestling with slippery pencils,
and leafing for "truth" in chunks of coarse paper;
Rosie, who stayed after school
"to sweep the floor"
and sprinkle water on the dust of thirty feet;
Rosie, spawning gossip
for those after-breakfast women
grouped in the only village store;
pretty Sally Slade in June perfume
on the shafts of a January gibbous moon
and Sid walking her home
to the house out on Shale Point;
and jealous Sam Blane grinding teeth in the dark;
the fights in the gloom,
and the "shame" in the light;

Parson Ned
"dead set"
against "Halloween forms"
and "Christmas superstitions of stuff like Santa Claus,"
"No time to praise the Devil here
in Hemlock Cove;"
and "pillars of their community"
feared this boy
who gave their children
"little real work to do;"
burning outhouses in glorious "Bonfire Night"
and eventually a teacher to blame;
and the haunting nights when Sid pinched the candle out

in the school
and listened close to Sally
to the roaring surf way down the coast
past the dark granite caves
and the point;
the click of a latch in a fresh night breeze,
and the gossip again
when Sally moved away from the Cove
and the ominous babble of tongues...

"He's not the one"...
and the caplin curled on the beaches
in cameos of milky spawn and death...
"A teacher, that's a laugh!"...
and people turned over in their beds and slept,
and the gulls never cried at night...
"The day is coming when we'll have one,"...
and the white wooden church on Sand Hill
reflected in the waters
on calm, boatless Sundays
when fishermen had time to watch...
and the stained-glass Christ with lambs
a glory in every peeping sunrise
when no men saw within...
"Taking our children into the woods
and telling them that a rock
in the pool of the brook
is an island,"...
and the small river wore deeper
into the shale valley of the Cove,
and carried the seasons...

"Reading stuff by poets with queer ideas
like men are islands and such,"...

and wayward snows swept by frosty windows
outside small stacks of dusty books
in ancient trunks forgotten…
"We'll have to put up with what we gets, I spose,"…
and the teacher skated with boys on a frozen pond;
the sun shone out there,
and the moon refused to burn…
"They'll never cover their books this way!"…
and the indifferent ocean cast layers
of glistening sand high up on the beach,
and scraped others away…
"Sam Blane says he works late at night
burning our oil in the school;
what's he doing up there?"…
"Old Emily complains of his late hours too…"
Soon the winds were finally whispering June again
and a home somewhere…

Sid left on a soft night in June
when the leaves were smelling of rain,
and a sheen of pebbles in the sky
made it slippery underfoot.
The steamer was late,
but it came in the night
and lingered on the swell outside the gut.
Two fishermen waited
to row Sid out - - - -

and bid farewell in the face of the steamer's light.
He climbed up a plank-ladder
with his suitcase gripped tight;
the steamer churned the Summer night,
and was gone.
The two returned

to sleeping Hemlock Cove.
The wind seems low tonight,
that coastal wind making men remember…
but listen,
listen…

THE TRAPPER

He told of that first rabbit
he saw his father catch
in a wire snare,
old wire stretched thin
and hairy in spots
like that long grey cord
holding their big picture
of World War One
in all those years
of upstairs halls.

He walked behind father
that winter morning
across still berry bushes
pressed under one snowfall
and across three ponds
that touched each other
with brook veins
slow under dark ice
and leaning alders
looped between the white earth
and the grey sky.

That rabbit cried
like a human,
like little brother
who had cried that morning
to come with them.
After father broke the neck
the woods were still.

He laughed at the thought
of father's promise
to little brother that morning
of how it was his turn
to have one of the hind legs
in supper gravy that night,
and be permitted
to cut pictures of planes
from those magazines
Aunt Becky sent
wired in bundles
from overseas.

The berry bushes tried to rise
in his father's footsteps
as they walked back
across one day's snow
and three silent ponds,
carrying a stiff rabbit
through the frozen loops
of the alder clump.

THE CELLAR

In the grey flurry light
of a winter morning
the root-cellar is snowed in
with long drifts carved
on its corners
facing the sea
and halfway up the door
of a full white painted moon
closed on a trackless plain
tinted with shadows of drifts
and solitary stalks of grass
and three grey stakes
once used to support a fence.

Behind the cellar
the sloping field
rises into the horizon of snow-light
and somewhere
below this line of meeting
the ocean can be heard
rising over rows of polished stones
below six grey stakes
once used to support a fence.

ISHMAEL

On the day he lay dying
in some little seaside town
he was left alone
in a dark upstairs room
behind pulled fly-spit blinds
that swayed as kelpy draughts came up
from an alley to the open sea.
This soft breeze tugged
at three clothes-pins
holding the blinds in place.
Two fat women
in that alley to the open sea
were talking about him
and his dying in the room above.
They were laughing at
"the talk he used to make"
of shipwrecks
white whales
and slender mermaids.
They giggled
in their maze of clothes-lines
wondering if
"he ever had a woman."
Occasionally one cursed as she searched
for more clothes-pins
to hold all the baby clothes
securely in place.

FROM THE LIGHTHOUSE

We found no keeper at the light.
It was now fully automated.
So we returned along old coastal roads
through rocky meadows in low fogs
where cattle stood still as the houses
in the moving, salt-mist sheen.
Men waved at us from piles of driftwood
behind grey picket-fences
across dark windows
on the shining clapboards.
Several times in the thick afternoon
sheep moved across the road
defying our headlights.
We drove past dark shops
where keepers sat on flour barrels
watching the rain fall on the road.
At one of the stores
where we stopped to buy matches
an old man fumbling through piles of boxes
told us about the first road
that used to go to the lighthouse.
He kept pointing out the window
to where it used to be
down through the rock-dotted meadows
sloping towards an ocean's sound.
And he jokingly complained
about his pet sheep always underfoot,
two of them asleep with a big black dog
beneath a rusty sign
once used for advertising flashlight batteries.

SCAPE

In the early winter on the snowless slopes
grey like old and salted fish-skin,
dark boulders perched on crystals of ice
defying the sun on screes above the pond
and the gravel-winds honed the landscape's edge.

Among the boulders stood three fishing shacks
mottled-white, with boarded-up windows and doors.
And dark, stained barrels with darker gaps of missing staves
leaned against the clapboards up there.

Below, I walked on the pond's clear ice
above six salmon on the mottled-grey silt,
defining themselves with movements of metal-sharp gills
deep down in the staves of tide-polished weeds.
And they would not move from my shadows or my stamping feet
as I tried all day to drive them away.

In that evening it snowed,
covering the slopes, the boulders, the barrels and all up there
but the gaping dark holes where the staves were gone.

Next day, I was glad of the definite white
as I walked across the pond's blank surface
between me and those six sluggish fish somewhere below.
And I left dark tracks to be soon erased by the winds.

NOAH

We could never regard him as one of us,
that little boy who made boats all summer
even though the puddle had dried up
and our town was miles from the sea.
He seemed to like the rain
when it did come,
that sissy who would sit inside
below his mother's breasts
reading story-books all day
and asking questions about the hills
above our town.
Once he came out near the end of a shower
and got all excited about some raven
flying across a rainbow.
He never killed frogs with us
when we sharpened summer spears
from the leafy twigs,
and he never owned a fishing pole.
Sometimes our parents made us
invite him to our birthday parties
and his parents forced him to come.
When he did arrive
he spent most of his time
staring through the window.
He was no comfort to any of us,
I can tell you that.

HOUSE ON THE COAST

There's a plain old house on a coast
with evening now in its upper panes
and no smoke in the on-shore air
to blur the lines
of seven sea-gulls wheeling
the horizon definite
over rock edges and pools
and the empty pebble-beach.
And one worn clothesline slants
towards a closed back-door.
And nobody takes the three figures
off the swaying line.

Nobody disturbs any of the lines
on this coast anymore
as all the lines etch deeper
into yesterday.

SCARECROW

For some strange reason
all the people have left the farm.
A scarecrow looms in the kitchen-garden
and all birds keep distance
in the purple hills.
A sun blazes down
on a straw-stuffed skull of flour-sack
on a cross of old black wood.
An old woman's hat tilts on the skyline.
A tattered grandfather scarf
chokes a purple robe
holding on
to one child's fluttering glove.
A pair of men's army pants
hang footless in the breeze
down from those purple hills
where the birds are silent.
And there is one other garment
fallen from the cross of black wood
deep in the long brown drills.
Under the coming green leaves
the strawberries will burst blood-red
and cover those several black feathers
lying dusty on the shade.

STORM COMING, WINTER AFTERNOON

Three crows drift across the sky
like discarded gloves
and fall suddenly into hazy woods
far beyond a well-house
with its door ajar.

Out in the frozen yard
a clothesline pole
swings back and forth
like a wild metronome.
Only stalks of the cut grass
seem to be still.

Across the vapour fields
that once waved in August
the thirsty scythe-men
used to wave at me
coming to the well house
with their smooth, white jugs
and noons above the clothesline poles.
Once in that time
one of them stopped
and read my birthday book to me:
a fable from Aesop
about a crow and smooth pebbles
and a water-pitcher...

Now I cannot see the woods
through the drifting snow
and the well-house is lost
somewhere out there
where the clothesline strains

at its rusty pulleys
like a trapped bird
and the grass stalks
sink deeper in the shifting hollows.

DREAMING OF AN ALMOST-FORGOTTEN FRIEND

We were walking alone
my friend
just the two of us
along the country lane
in the land where I grew up
with picket fences
and meeting shadows of birches
above and below our walking.
I stopped and leaned on a fence
to watch the hills
rise up from the green-dung grass
and dwarf-spruce clinging to the rocks.
Up there where the timber was darkest
a waterfall trailed down
so narrow and white and long.
I had never seen the waterfall before.
We stopped to listen to its falling
hoping the wind and all was right.
But you stayed in the noise of leaves
and wind in branches behind me.
I kept saying how strange
how strange that water with no sound.
You only spoke to tell me
that the waterfall was frozen.

THE ANGLER

On many mornings
he comes ape-like
down the dawn-stained railway tracks
and approaches the lagoon
where the sea ebbs in
to the edges of big oil-tanks
fish-plant walls and warehouse sheds.

Each time he stands on the oily pebbles
with his back to the sheds
and casts his line into the sea.
Out there is his private hubris
in that misty-purple light
he knows the great trout
will still rise
for one in the dawntime.

Something tugs at his line
each time he reels in
his white-moth fly
from which he has carefully removed
the curved barb of a hook.

Each time he quietly leaves
before the workers come
before the sun rises
above the rows of factory roofs.

CONNECTIONS

When old birches bend leafless
in wild pawings
of the long night winds
we who lie
within our ease of walls
and man-shaped symmetry
never dare
to arise and go out there.
It's more comfortable to make analogies
and see those trees out there
as white and kind old men
as guardians of our tended lawns
like knotted benignity
in our children's books.

Some burning wood stirs
in a grate downstairs.
We know for sure
that our great wooden door
is locked down there.
And we can sleep through this night
if we group and connect
our comfortable similes and such
as stays against
disconnection.

TRIP

We fished all through the night,
my friend and I
casting silver lures
into a moon-scaled surf,
waiting for big sea-trout
to school on the rising tide.
But thousands of young smolt
kept hooking themselves
on our lures
and we kept cursing them
and throwing them back.
Behind us
on mounds of polished sea-stones
our driftweed fire winked.

Next evening, as we drove home
along slow coastline roads
through small villages,
groups of young women smiled
at our passing headlights
and silhouetted themselves
in snack-bar doorways
lit up by jukebox light.
Behind us
a full moon slid up
from curves of ash-coloured hills.

THE MADONNA

The island's last families
had sailed away
years ago
and left their church
on the fallow slopes.
Like a piece of sculpture
depicting watchfulness,
this church looked down
over empty, grey cottages
and a few uncertain sheds
that seemed to lean
with the whims of each wind.
And the high church walls
that seemed to be well-preserved
and shone in the coolness
of ephemeral, fog-released sunshines
above the creeping mists
still clinging to the ground.
These walls loomed strong
in the many days of northeast grey
and they never leaned
in any gale's direction
when wild grasses waved
around the white clapboards
as wind came up from catpaws
on the bight below.
And there were certain still nights
when the ocean pulsed in calm
and duplicated every-season's moon.
On such nights
the firm church-steeple seemed
to waver down on a ribbon of tide

and no wind chipped
sheets of white light
on the sable surface.
And time worked on
in the sun and the fog
and the moon and the tides
along passive edges
on the island....

One day in late September
in an afternoon of salt sun
and fast-sailing fluffs of cloud,
the church clapboards shone
like white marble on the drab landscape.
And long grasses nodded
in the open churchyard
of a few grey outcrops
and some easterly leaning tombstones.
Up on the dark felt roof of the church
a thin streak of white flowed down
from the chimney's form
where some gull had emptied its bowels.
And there were thin rust lines
flowing down across the clapboards
from old hinges in the window frames.
The heavy main-entrance door
was well-latched and unlocked
and through the afternoon
local breezes rattled lightly
on the metal tongue of the latch
and gull-shadows drifted
across the sunlight
on the western clapboards...

Inside the church,
light fell from the western windows
magnifying myriad grains of dust
in undulating patterns
across the brown pews
and narrow, empty aisles.
And the wind moved up in the rafters
above old metal spans
where paint had never been applied.
The Madonna was one of the few
things left behind
in the days when the people left.
This white, marble statue
stood in varnished shadows
off to the right of the altar.
Life-size, she smiled serenely
at the eastern wall
from her radiant curves
of robe like the sea-bird's wing.
Occasionally, a cloud passed by the sun
and the dust-lines of light
disappeared across the pews
and the shadows deepened fitfully
where the Madonna stood
with her great sculpted garments
winding to the bare wooden floor...

Down in the afternoon bight,
two teenage boys were moving on the shoreline,
along the mounds of granite pebbles,
moving slowly up the slopes
toward the churchyard.
They had arrived in the late morning
and beached an orange, fiberglass boat

high up from the landwash
and the rising tide.
The gaudy craft was held
by a tapering nylon rope
wrapped in clumsy knots
around a beak-like projection
of an ancient schooner-spar
sticking up through the pebbles
where the beach met the uncut meadows.
Side by side along the beach crest
they kept moving
barely stopping at all on the drumlins
of the barren slopes
as if they knew where they were going.
Out on the ultramarine blue
of the autumn-sheened bay,
a big school of mackerel
pushed a van of spray
into the face of the breeze.
One of the boys watched the fish
with his powerful binoculars
and adjusted himself behind the cross
of leather straps
from these glasses and an expensive camera.
His friend carried a small rifle
and pumped thee shots
out into the moving school.
"Why waste good lead?"
asked the gunner's friend.
"We got lots," the other replied,
"my arse pockets are full."
And he patted his back pockets
bulging tight across his "go-go" buttocks.
"Is it true what they say

about these mackerel fish…
that they have to keep moving
or they die?"

"Yes. Moving to keep living. That's right,
just like every bloody soul
who lived here on this island
had to do."

They both seemed pleased
with their analogy
and laughed aloud as they hurried
up the island's contours…

Up inside the old church,
the smiling Madonna still watched
the still sunlight
on the eastern wall
where all was quiet
except for fluttering winds
high up in the grey, cool rafters…

"Not a bad place on a day like this,
but I wouldn't live here
all through winter.
No wonder they moved away!"

"The sea is blue now, right?"

"Sure. What are you getting at?"

"Remember our old art teacher?"

"Yeah. 'Old Tints' we called him."

"Remember how he preached at us
about that Dutch artist

who sliced off his ear
and gave it to some old bag?"

"Yeah. Boy what we suffered
until we made a joke of him."

"Remember how he used to tell
us to mix our colours more
whenever we painted the sea?
To him it was never just blue.
Remember how he talked about that painter,
Van something-or-other
who saw the sea like a mackerel skin,
a lot of colours all mixed?"

"Yeah. But look at the sea out there.
Looks only blue to me."

"Same here."

The boy with the gun almost whispered
as he spoke:
"Speaking of moving to stay alive,
that gull better keep on moving."
He was aiming the riffle at a saddleback,
poised in white grace
and gliding on the updraught
of the coastline…
The crack of the rifle echoed
from the eastern cliffs of the beach
and a wraith of grey smoke
puffed from the barrel

and dissipated quickly on the breeze.
As the bullet smashed the gull's rib-cage,

several big feathers splayed
on a blob of red
and a gush of guano
trailed a white line down
across the screen of sea and sky.
The great wings seemed to fold inward
before the death plunge
into the kelp-ringed crags
at the base of the eastern cliffs.

The boys ran towards the fall
but soon they stopped
because it was too far away.
One of them peered with the binoculars.

"A darn good shot. You sure sent his guts
and feathers flying."

"Yeah. He's a mess now
that I don't want to see."

"How do you know that bird is a he?"

"Oh, come on, for God's sake keep moving.
I'm in a hurry, come on,
keep moving if you want to live."

"Don't point that gun at me!"
I'll go back to the boat, I will!"

"Come on then," shouted the gunner playfully.
They both laughed and sang
and the gunner followed his friend
in mock pursuit
up the long, fall slopes

of the forsaken community.
Inside the crossed leather-straps
of glasses and camera
the leader puffed and gasped for breath
on the steepest contours of the island…

They approached the long grasses
of the churchyard
where brown sparrows darted up
from among fallen fences and mounds.
Wandering around the weathered stones,
the boys impatiently marched
toward the entrance of the church.
A gull's shadow blew rapidly
across the grass
in front of them
as they neared the old stone steps.
The old latch was raised
and the door pushed in
and they paused before entry…

"Hey, this must be the old Catholic church."

"Yeah. Remember how old Aunt Mary
use to warn us about their images
and statues and other weird things?"

Moving into the porch of dusty emptiness,
they made sure the door stayed open
on back of them.
And they moved up the empty aisles
across the lines of sunlight
from the row of western windows.
They approached the altar…

"I used to be afraid
to pass the Catholic church
after dark by myself,
though it was only a gunshot
from our own."

"Come on, let's go back outside."

"Are you afraid of those people
who used to talk to statues?"

"No. But this gives me the creeps."

"Wait. Don't go yet. I want to help the wind
tear down this place."

He shot three small holes into the windows
of the eastern wall
and six into the panes
along the west.
The glass did not shatter immediately
but left small, distinct patterns
to be worked on by the wind.

"Come on. You'll find some gulls
outside to shoot
or something...I'm going...
see you outside...."

"No wait. Look, there's the Virgin herself."
The gunner backed down the aisle
to keep close to his friend
who was going through the door.
As he backed away
across the lines of sunlight

he fired several shots
at the smiling Madonna
poised gracefully in the shadows.
Some shots missed her wing-like contours.
But others etched dark spider-marks
along the marble framework.
One bullet punched near the eye
and fine particles trickled
into the dark shadows near her feet
of feathered stone.
She still smiled gently
below the now-marred eye…

In great haste, the boys had gone
and slammed the great door shut.
Far up the slopes
above the churchyard
they were running silhouettes now
zig-zagging on the moving sky…

Hours later, they were heading down
towards their waiting boat
where the tide had come in.
It was easy now to sail
out of the bight.
As the orange craft glided away
some voices came in on the breeze
piecemeal:
"I've used all my shots."
"Give me those oars!"
"Free, free, like a bird on the blue, blue sea."
"I did not take a single picture…"
"Keep moving…keep moving…"
And they were gone

around the headland;
laughter…parts of a song…and…
distant voice…

That evening, up in the church,
as the wind moaned in the eaves,
a piece of glass fell from the western rows.
The Madonna stood in deep shadow now,
still smiling at the eastern wall,
a wall now tinged with deep orange.
Somewhere, far above the dark felt roof,
a gull screamed savagely.

Down on the crags where the bird-carcass lay,
the sea had become choppy.
Down across the beach-rocks,
An empty rifle-shell clattered
on a gust of wind.

That night, inside the church,
another piece of glass fell
from the middle window
of the eastern wall
and rattled sharply
across the cool darkness
of the wooden floor.

SOMETHING GONE

Something had left me waiting
alone inside an old house under elms.
And the wires of November showers
crossed the bay-windows
and connected skies and leaves
and dripping, unpainted eaves.

Through the long, blurred windows
I watched
lines of harvested potato fields
brown and puddle-dotted
beyond the distant border
of a country road.

Somewhere between the showers
clumps of small birds
preened themselves on the drooping wires
of a rickety pole-line.

Inside the house
from time to time
I stared at the quaint telephone.
It waited
coiled coldly
like some black hieroglyphic
perched on the rain-stained wall.

BY THE TRACKS

I used to sleep
in that house
by the railway tracks
where the night-train
never crept by.
Some nights its noise came
like a rush of war planes
and drew me frightened from my bed
to the window
thinking of the Cuban crisis
Berlin and shelter in the basement.
It was beautiful going back to bed.

I am back in that house again
by the railway tracks
where the night-train
goes no more.
One night I walked in my sleep
and awoke at the window.
The moon was a broken yoke
that flowed from the clouds
into the weeds growing high
between the warped sleepers.
I could not go back to bed again.

BIRTH CONTROL

Many poets
chew the pill
of modern society
but many more are forced to swallow it.
Ingredients:
nineteen hundred and so many
grains of conformity;
average acids;
plus a new active agent
of formal education;
pure powder of pace
in a matrix of computer's milk.
Too often
this pill
controls the birth
of poems.

CHILDREN IN THE ALLEY

Our feuding families
sleep
unseen behind their metal blinds.
We, the children,
know it is dusk.
We come out to play
in the darkening street,
each staring over his shoulder
at luminous numbers
nailed on the door-posts.
Overhead
the dinosaurs
sprouting from chimneys
somewhere
in the drain-pipe evening
drift.
We are the alley children
who love each other.
What Passover is to come?
Are we blood
on the door-posts?

THE LITTLE MAN

A class and I must talk of Gulliver
in Brobdingnag
and some may think
I stretch a leg
or am strangely lonely
to say this tale
is not for children only....

From the dusty circle of a button-hole
I'm peeping up
and back
as a frigid, first-day boy
at school again...
afraid
of towering, yellow-green pencil weeds
and sharp crayons of grass
marking and chopping
the horizon
of scribbler-paper light...
Somebody prods me
with a finger-ladder
down from the forest of eyes
and with insect haste
I scurry under
somebody carrying a number...
and I'm lost
somewhere
between the apple
and the rule.

BABEL

When the plains were lush
in the lines of after-rain sun,
the engineers were one
in talking of plans for prosperity.
And it came to pass
that their great building towered
into the moving sky.
But there were workers in the basement
who whispered of rumours
that the engineers had argued
on the safety of foundation spans;
and millions of worried faces
flicked up and down in elevators each day
always hurrying and watching clocks
and looking as if somebody
did not understand them;
and there were suicides from top stories
often leaving notes to explain something;
and grumpy janitors pushed big brooms
at the heels of "big shots" working late;
and pretty secretaries frowned
and carried orders from computers
behind closed doors.
Sometimes in the long corridors
children marked messages in crayon
and passing voices wondered
what was "getting into kids today."
And on through miles of night
stretched the on-and-off geometry
of window lights.
And in grey days on the concrete plains
in the oil-lined clouds
the building seemed to lean.

1965–1985

UNCOLLECTED

THE SCULPIN

A grotesque fish
he wobbled savagely
up from the nether jungle
of undulating ocean floor
as if the bottom had given
a piece of itself
to gulp the noon-day hook
of a careless, unsuspecting boy
who had eyes for only
oily streaks of
bark-like tom-cod
and dish-blue connors
that slyly lingered.

Now in the smells and sounds
of a summer wharf
he twisted and thumped
away his life
on splintered boards
and cruel heads of nails
beneath the kicks
and scuffs of those
who cared not
if he died.

An energetic tourist
told his wife to come
and see the devil
while the wharf boys
tried to act indifferently
in front of the alien form
of a pink-dressed woman

wearing a flower
and fussing like someone
faking fear.

Soon all went home
to waiting dinners.
The dead sculpin's body
was anchored in a crust
of sun-baked slime.
Big distinguished flies
walked fitfully
over his horny head
and swarmed
in patch-like clusters
on his lower lip.

In their buzzing
the wharf was seeming quiet
except for the pervading slap
of water on driven piles
and sea-gull screams
bursting from behind high
drifting clouds
to vie the murmurs
from the lazy hinterland.

An old man
perhaps unable to go to sea again
apart from the distance
of the wharf's projection
sat on a cod-oil coloured tub
upturned near the edge.

He gazed upwardly outward

into the four o'clock haze
and blinked for five
shimmering minutes.
He looked down only once
and turned over the sculpin
with his shaking walking stick.

He saw the paper-wrinkled belly
which made the form look
like a fish at last.

The old man left.
A little girl almost saw
the lifeless fish
through her five o'clock eyes
but her mother warned her
to come back.

She might have felt his wounds
but her daddy was coming home
to supper.

Nobody came again till after supper
then they came
and left again
with their heavy strings
of other fish
while the neglected sculpin
received an evening drizzle
of forming rain.

Nobody ever saw again
the staggering village drunkard.
He would never know
what caused him to slip and fall.

Both man and sculpin
late that night
were caught by the undertow
and that was all.

(1965)

DOG-FISH SUMMER

Cruel were the days
when tired hearts became
empty as erosioned hands
and inherent salt
began to leave
the once-exuberant blood
of grown men crying
in faded oil-skins
and praying
and cursing
in the face of
a sand-paper sky
while anxious kin waited
existingly
walking the margins
and peering through
crusted eyes.

Such was the distant summer
of thirty-five
when Uncle Tim
the village fool
tried to stay alive
and day after empty day
ripped baneful dog-fish
from his four frayed trawls
and all but gave up
waiting for Luck
who each day stayed
with the careless boy
back on the rock-dry wharf

catching the willing connors.
Some people forced themselves
to care
for Uncle Tim
and others pretended to care
for him
but he bore a heavy cross
up a dusty road
from an empty indifferent boat.
He heard them laugh
from the molasses-shade
of the general store
while the girl-conscious
young men "funned" with him
where Luck was
but the old man
thought of others
and his mother speaking
from the sunny shadows
of a Sunday evening:
"What of the promise of his coming?"
He walked this dreadful road
with pitiful patience
because another fisherman
had one day
walked the briny waves
and now hung
on his bedroom wall.
Uncle Tim had finally
sweat his way up the dusty hill
as he leaned on
the crutches of memory
and watched dirty little boys

dragging passive dog-fish
through the sand.
Those streaks of shark
were stinking on the beach
as they rotted
in the maw of
the August swell
pulsing half-digestedly.

Each day the dreaded ritual
each night the hopeful dreams
and always
now it seemed
pervading all,
the dog-fish.

One day in early ripe September
Uncle Tim smelled promise
in the wind that blew
fragrantly off-shore
out towards the grounds
and shouting above the cries
of screaming sea-gulls
asked one of the little boys
if he wished
to come
with him.

On this day
boy and old man
hauled cod after cod
from four rejuvenated trawls.
Those bread fish
beat out their lives

in a mess of blood
and skin-shine
on the sun-browned
dory floor.
They flapped and thumped
as the two
kept hauling
and filling the boat.
From deep down
the great half-light
blotches came
and kept coming
and coming
and the old man knew
he had his good-luck charm
and the boy
wanted to be his luck
to return with the old man
and be by his side
when he shut the village mouths
and opened them
in other tones
and talk.
Tonight the sleep
would be deep
and sweet
as Uncle Tim longed
for tomorrow.

However, when the new day came
the father of the boy
came angrily to the shore
a man of little faith
he tried

to snatch his son away
while in the space of seconds
Uncle Tim returned once more
to the Sunday shadows
and his mother's quavering voice:
"O, ye of little faith!"
In a painful flash
the old man swung his
primitive gaff
and ripped it back
after its rusty-iron tip
had bashed the father's head
and the man lay
bleeding in the landwash
surprised
with what life he had left
to be surprised with
and to gaze into the
mad eyes of the village fool.
He would soon give up the ghost
the father would die
the son
would be taken.

Looking at blood returning
to the salt
the old man grabbed
the crying child
and threw him into
the boat of yesterday's
slimy luck
and madly skimmed
for the fishing grounds.

But today the cod had gone
and the sand-paper sky
invaded the ocean
and the sand-paper fish
were back
black-deep and hook-hungry
and four frayed trawls
were full of them.
Uncle Tim cursed at the sky again
then prayed and looked back
at the land.

(1968)

APPARITION

Late singular evening
through a pane of frost
in a sick-boy window
of a winter now lost
I saw a dark cat stalking
across a down
of newly fallen snow
and padded paws punched
little eye-like tracks
as the apparition
carried someone's kitchen
over the passive plain
as new flakes filled
the tracks
and eyes again.
It squeezed its greying mat
beneath the fence
and drifted dark into the barbs
and waiting specter trees.
The wraith wound savage
in the evening spool
had left the warm kitchen
with the two
of me.

(1969)

FEATHERS

Feathers falling in the night
whispers of souls on the stairs
displacing nothing
but themselves
to fall in place again
tracing a graph
on the skin of the sky unseen
and striking the ground
with a sound beyond
the range of man.

Inky pigeon parks
and pens of gull
across a page of coast
write some message
in the sands.

I remember one night
beyond the city sounds
yet within the iron quills
of its park
I walked on feathers
in the dark
and thought of Icarus.

(1969)

SNOW-POEM SUGGESTION

I've stopped being so precise
about the poetry of snow
falling first
in fumbling flakes
each year.
Elusive herds
I fail
to fence within
with words:
they quiver in dusks
over drumlins here
and pigeon eaves
and distances unseen
all drops
to melt untouched
in palms of pallid leaves
outposted
worlds within worlds
everything
uncaptured.

(1970)

A FAREWELL TO ARMS

You must notice
how the sparrows came
at twilight
and flittered around
the defining eaves.
As darkness deepened
and made defining difficult
the nighthawks came.
You must notice also
how a bat flew in
and hunted something
as if the unlit room
was not defined by walls.

This is Hemingway
on love and war.
It's more than lovers
bedding their time
and listening
to armies
somewhere
in an opaque distance
through an open window.

(1972)

CHILDREN FROM PORLOCK

Every poet should know that
the man from Porlock
became a father.
At that moment of poetic dawn
his children could come
stepping rapidly on the stones
across your silences.
They will come
with voices chiseling the first light,
in their folds of calendar clothes
on time-piece feet.
You too
could be called out
by them.

That tapping on your door
is not always the rain
or something carried in the wind
where you are sleeping.

(1972)

OTTAWA OCTOBER CRISIS, 1970

Pan was running
in our woods again
last night.
The watery dawn
will let fall
the leaves of his piping night
to be measured
by the rakings of the day
drifting out from deep groves
and across concrete walks.
Caretakers
are now permitted
to burn them again.
But troops pace slowly
in the quiet smoke.

(1972)

MONDAY MORNING

It kept mattering
that wet winds
rattled the window panes
all night from
a splashing, street-light west
somewhere beyond
a blue-line of brick
and came rushing through
those darkest morning hours
like the trees were walking.
Drops of light
spilled from the focusing eaves
falling wake
wake
wake.

I yawned
counting
six yellow leaves
and a scrap of newspaper
stuck on a mottled window pane.

(1972)

GULLS AND ICE

The harbour
once ice-congested
succumbed to an Arctic thrust
and threw its margins
upwards jaggedly
to pierce the eggshell horizon
undulating the whole
on immaculate whites
and close-up watery greens
in a matrix
of melting spring sky
seeming to cast itself
gracefully awry
in wheels of wavering flight
as sea gulls
in a new-creation light.

(1972)

SUMMER WAS

Summer was
where the splashing brook came from
along cool black-mossed stones
that felt like swimming dogs.

Summer was
under the greens of wasp shades
in long dog-day suns.

We came out of those shades
to where the brook slid
under new, dry pavement.
Along this smooth surface
on our way to soda-fountains
the heat-waves over asphalt skin
shaped mirages of those clear brook pools
we could always walk back to find.

And the water came to pass
under the metal rows of oil-tanks
near the metered lot
where we were taught
to drive cars.

(1972)

SUMMER OF FORTY SOMETHING-OR-OTHER

Somewhere in that summer vortex
father went away once
as the sun was pulled down
and no rain fell for moon long;
the river's peels swirled shallow
and big trout with bulging eyes
swung choking to the surface
into my little brother's hands
in these days of suns
like shining coppers
when a little boy died up the road
and lay all dressed with coins on his eyes.
A young man drove in from the city
to court our aunt away;
he stood watching the china clock
while she was somewhere dressing
and mother, swirling grease around a fry-pan,
told him about the easy trout
and he gave us cents for bubble-gum,
my brother and myself,
as grandfather cursed the radio,
turning a big brown button
to the news from overseas.

(1972)

EVENING, SIGNAL HILL

Up here on the dark north wind
I cannot see
the clumps of stained grass
seeking cover in deep faults of stone.
Off into the eastern void of fog
between Europe and myself
a needle-point of light
seems moving closer.
Down on the southern point of rock
some solitary light-pulse throbs
in case of ships.
And on the flushed fog
in the west below
a city is disconnected
dots of light.
I turn from the city
and look to the salted east again
where there are fewer dots to connect
and fewer games
from the starting point of me.

(1973)

IN THERE SOMEWHERE

"What if the Beothuks are not all dead?
Suppose a group of them
were wise enough to hide
somewhere deep in the island's interior?"

"Just think...
they could still be
in there somewhere!"

Somebody laughs at her
and it rattles like the chains
of beaver traps.

I could not laugh
at what the lady tourist said.
Why should I scorn
a little ignorance
(or call it what you will)
of Newfoundland geography.

Besides, I know that
deep within my island
there are austere voices
in the August birch
and slow dawns are caught
in great wooden bowls
where the meek shall inherit.
And a moon is always
a moving canoe
across blue acres of the night.

And a child is always
laughing
in the splash of white water
down the long bakeapple hills.

I could not laugh
because they are
still
in there
somewhere.

(1978)

ON THE FULL TIDE

Returning
returning as the tide
pulled down the twilight
the man at the rudder
ceased to be
the one who scorned you
for your soft, white hands
holding the thorns from lobster pots
and wrinkled like iced kelp
across the nets of fall,
the one who warned you
about the sin and bad luck
of whistling on the water,
the one who swore
that you'd never be a man.
In the returning time,
returning with the rising tide,
he was always quiet
as a dark pinnacle
against the white boat wake.
I was happy in this genesis
to feel that he was listening
as I was listening:

to clean surf on the angel rocks
and sea-birds calling
from the silver folds of landwash,
and rushing rivers sounding on the prow
and streaming from the cliffs
far up above us,
and happy children's voices

defining the dark void
of the headland.
I always felt that
he smiled at me then
as the pure surf smiled at me,
in the ringing cliffs as the sea-birds
as the children smiled at me.
And it was good.

(1979)

IN THE HEART OF THE COUNTRY

I trapped in my younger days,
trapped everything.
It was hard at first,
all the blood and suffering.
But I kept telling myself
it was just a living,
so I got used to it.

When we were youngsters,
the weasel frightened everybody.
If it turned up, the men ran
for their guns, and the women
made sure we were all inside.
Small as it was,
it came straight from the devil,
like a snake,
and its spit was poison.
Those old beliefs
stayed with me years later
up in the woods
by myself.

One night, alone in a tilt,
I sat up suddenly in my sleep.
I'd been dreaming a bird
was singing somewhere
in the dead dark. I waited
as everything got quiet.
No sound but my pocket-watch ticking.
It struck me I was further in
than ever before,

in country where the water
ran the other way.

And queer things go through your head
in the woods at night.
There was no bird singing.
A weasel was chirping
in the wall behind my head.
I was in its territory now.
I waited. And waited...

Suddenly, just like that,
I knew the beast
in the village
was really inside our heads.

I took a deep breath, settling back.
Outside, the wind murmured
and water whispered the other way.
My pocket-watch ticked on.
Once in awhile the weasel stirred,
chirping softly
inside the mossy walls.
In the heart of the country
I'd never be uneasy again.

(1981)

LEAH

Shouldn't be too long now, he's gone
down the coast again, she said,
putting the kettle on.
I was a young fellow,
a folklore student from the city,
there to record her husband's stories.
But he never showed up
and the afternoon wore on.
I'd have to be getting back to town soon.

I wish he'd stop going out in the boat by himself,
she complained, standing by the kitchen window.
I heard waves combing the beach below.
Nobody lives there anymore, she added.

A wonderful hand for the girls he was,
when he was young, she said, half smiling,
but he picked me over all of them. I wasn't
the nicest looking one, still...he picked me.

She had a story of her own,
but she was telling it piecemeal.
I didn't turn on the tape recorder.
She turned from the window.

They were the dainty, prissy ones, she said,
but I could do men's work too, spreading fish and whatever.
One of them, a teacher, is buried down there.
He goes back there every chance he gets,
to catch a trout or set a few snares.
Brings back a turn of birch sometimes.
Says he's never lonesome there by himself.

Still, I'm worn out thinking about him.
Anything could happen.
He's not up to it anymore.

Later, as I was leaving,
she stood on the bridge,
slowly shaking her head.
He's usually back by now, she said,
I hope nothing happened.

(circa 1981)

SOLE SURVIVOR

He owns it all now, the big house, acres of land.
Everyone in the community said he was soft, naive,
that the merchant played him for a fool.
Had he kept a diary, it might have made interesting reading,
but he lived in an age when diaries and activities like gardening
were left to women. Men would never show feelings like that.
Everybody knew how he was tricked into marrying Sarah,
she who was carrying the merchant's child.
One day you will own it all, the merchant had told him.

After all the years, he's alone in the big house now,
still whispered about. Perhaps he's changed somewhat.
Might even be keeping a diary. He's old now,
mumbles to himself a bit. Spends his winters
down south, coming back with ideas for his garden.
He's sure the merchant would be pleased
with the way he's kept up appearances.

(circa 1982)

THE SIGNS

South-West Brook is loud tonight,
a sign of rain,
Grandfather said.
See that ring around the moon?
The moon is sick, my son,
a storm for sure.

We were walking home
in the landwash
and I reached up
to hold his hand.
It was very dark.
Look close, he said,
out over the water.
We might see the lights
of the "Effie-Jane"
lost years ago, he whispered.

Look, there she goes, he said.
See that little peck out there?
I squinted hard
but I couldn't see anything.
We were silent
for the rest of the way home.

Next day it was so stormy
I sat at the window dreaming,
smelling the Devil in the chimney.
Two out of three
wasn't bad, I thought.

(circa 1983)

HAIKU SELECTIONS

West Country cemetery
a Hardy rain
erasing names

after Beethoven
stars and crickets
carry on

again the owl...
distance
questioning

abandoned lighthouse
going up steps
              shellwise

after Kazantzakis
god
in the ant's
black
eye
watching
me

long after
the cat
 silence
 lingers
 on the window sill

misty twilight
so many summers
in a snipe's winnow

suspended
from fiddlehead
august spider
in search
of another
sun

imagining
a green
lane
where Blake
struck the sky
with an alder
stick

Good Friday
snow flurry
light
over porch door
left on
all day

APPENDIX: ORIGINAL CONTENTS

The following lists reproduce, chronologically, the complete tables of contents from each of Dawe's first three full-length collections, since their appearance and sequence in *New and Collected Poems* differ from the original publications. The symbols which occur next to individual poems indicate where these poems subsequently appeared, and thus their location in *New and Collected Poems*.

In Hardy Country *
Where Genesis Begins †

HEMLOCK COVE AND AFTER

A Day in '45*
Inuk
The Watcher*
Stranger at Hemlock Cove
Outport Christmas*
The Trapper
The Old Man and the Moon*
The Cellar
Ishmael
From the Lighthouse
Scape
Noah
House on the Coast
Vortex*
Stage*
Scarecrow
Storm Coming, Winter Afternoon
Dark Morning*
Dreaming of an Almost Forgotten Friend
The Angler
Pages †
Connections

Trip
The Madonna
Something Gone
By the Tracks
Birth Control
Children in the Alley
The Little Man
Babel
The Bear*
Calling the Children*

ISLAND SPELL

Ghosts
A Fairy Tale*
The Far Island
The Dead Boy*
The Potato Ground
Interval
Once by the Atlantic
The Scythe
White Horses
In a Small Cove*
The Naked Man*
The Guitar Player
Along that Coast
The Stranger
Abandoned Outport*
A Consecration*
Evening, Bareneed, Conception Bay*
At Western Arm*
In Picasso's "Madman"*
Three in the Summer Afternoon
Ishmael Remembers
Ishmael Remembers (2)
Peggy*
The Bridge
The Mummer*
Beach Moments, September '56

The Headland
The Bogey Man*
The Veteran*
The Veteran (2)*
The Veteran (3)
Low Tide
Poor Peter
Once After Sunday
To a Poet

IN HARDY COUNTRY

In Hardy Country
A Fairy Tale
Riddle
Still Life
Devil at the Dance
The Bogey Man
Solstice, Outport Childhood
Uncle
Peppermint Rock
One Fall Night
Outport Christmas
On Small Island
Boatman
Caretaker
A Day In '45
The Dead Boy
Summerplace
Abandoned Outport
At Western Arm
Dark Morning
The Mummer
The Old Man and the Moon
Figures from Ancestral Landscape
The Bear
Communion
Evening, Bareneed, Conception Bay
The Watcher

The Naked Man
The Widow and the Butcher Boy
Peggy
Marsh
Vortex
Cape Shore Woman
Stage
Top of the World
A Consecration
In A Small Cove
The French Shore Man
Bonfire Night
The Ballad of Flora
In Picasso's "Madman"
Haiku (1)
Haiku (2)
Haiku (3)
Haiku (4)
Haiku (5)
On Cuslett Brook (1979)
Edwardians (Old Photograph)
Back Road
The Veteran (1)
The Veteran (2)
Wild Geese
Sandpiper
If Sonnets Were In Fashion
"Struggle Into Light": A Poem to John Clare
Alders
Methodists
Bitch
Calling the Children
Daedalus
Daedalus at Garden Wall
Seabird
Salmon †
Hide and Seek

INDEX OF FIRST LINES

A bee is droning, 265
A class and I must talk of Gulliver, 328
A cold wind, 183
A grotesque fish, 333
A phantom ship drifts by, 174
A simple abode. Utensils few, 109
A struggle into light, 226
abandoned cove, ("North Light"), 68
abandoned cove, ("The Way"), 39
abandoned lighthouse, 367
abandoned orchard, 66
Above grey beach stones, 271
Above the headland, 272
According to legend, 139
after Beethoven, 365
after Kazantzakis, 368
after northeaster, 213
after the storm, 108
after your "Summer", 41
again the owl..., 366
alone on the barrens, 19
Alone on the beach this morning, 235
Another March day had died, 283
As I walk by the house tonight, 217
aspen, 171
At a garage sale this morning, 51
At my father's wake, men talked, 57

Back home now, 192
Back in that forever, 162
Back in the Romantic Age, 62
biology lab, 37

Caligula, wise man of course, 124
cliff-top tuckamore, 212
close-up, 40
Coppers on his eyes, 170
Cruel were the days, 337

dawn flecks, 210
deep snowfall, 158
Don Marquis once said, 55
Don't dwell on Nero's bloody rule, 123
dusty parlour, 114

Every poet should know that, 347
Experts will point out, correctly, that the Beothuk, 43

Feathers falling in the night, 344
Flat character. Cutout, 121
For me, it's no county overseas, 147
For some strange reason, 306
For them it is always Sunday afternoon, 216
Found this afternoon, 199
From the fall of the wind, 153

God's secret service is inscrutable, 126
Good Friday, 373

He has kept a light, 135
He owns it all now, the big house, acres of land, 362
He told of that first rabbit, 298
He was a few years older than the rest of us, 110
He was always, 156

I remember the year, 31
I trapped in my younger days, 358
I am the child of the original story, 112
I call out, 78
I don't know how we stood it all. Childhood
was all work, drudgery, 44
I don't remember much about that day, 278
I dreamed about Hemlock Cove, 266

I have no argument at all, 98
I know that I, 102
I lived as a child then, 169
I remember crowds of strangers, 267
I remember the last years of poor Peter, 275
I remember: cow-bells waking me, 247
I see them in summer, 151
I thought of you today, 89
I used to sleep, 325
I was once the best mummer, 175
I was taking my time, 165
I'd just finished my lecture on Conrad, 45
I'll not forget that foreign scene, 219
I've heard it all before, 167
I've stopped being so precise, 345
If somebody asked me, 160
If sonnets were in fashion, 224
imagining, 372
In a faint memory of '52, 182
In a poem, 48
In a porthole orb of light, 99
In a saltbox house under February stars, 33
In a wet August day, 185
In April the Easter snow came, 250
In many and various ways, creators, 26
In our hippie days, 24
In scattered folios, 128
In that long-gone summer, 259
In the early winter on the snowless slopes, 303
In the grey flurry light, 300
It kept mattering, 349
It happened at the Viking site one afternoon, 25
It hopped, 223
It is a Sabbath evening, 230
It was an August evening, 241
It was said, 261
It was the last place he wanted to be that night, 27

Just the three of us fishing there, 215
Just the two of us, 83

larksong, 65
Last night I dreamed, 229
Late singular evening, 343
Listen to the whisper of the night-wind, 289
listening, 46
long after, 369
Loren Eiseley once said, 142
Luke remembered, 201
lying in alders, 214

Many poets, 326
misty twilight, 370
Mornings alone, abstracted, 137
musing, 38
My cousin wasn't overseas, 273
My great grandmother, 149
My mother, who grew up on a farm, had an explanation, 61

No putt putt of the motor boat, 198
northern dawn, 54
northern El Greco, 69
Now in late November, 249

Old Man Coyote, 73
On fine, wire waves, 274
On goat-tramped hills, 86
On many mornings, 310
On path moss, 164
On the day he lay dying, 301
On the day when I finished this wall, 238
Once a year, at least, 163
Once in a long gone time, 179
Once in a mind-over-matter spell, 107
Once in Hemlock Cove, 184
Once looking for the sheep with father, 277
Once we had a wooden bridge, 269

one for sorrow, 34
Otters in a pool, 75
Our feuding families, 327
Out from a droke of woods, 22
Out in sable winds, 258

Paddy's comin' in a sleigh, 187
Pan was running, 348
People always went to Ishmael's for essentials, 103
Perhaps the man in the hayfield, 263
prayer flag, 67
precious pagan, 21

Quick stray snowflakes, 205

Resplendent in the ranks of mud, 100
Returning, 356
Riggs always waited for the Lord's Day, 105
Rumpelstiltskin will remain, 49

Saltbox house, 118
Seems I can mind them, 203
shards of sea glass, 47
She appeared in the season of small leaves, 232
She believes in God, 60
Sheer cliffs in sea-song, 202
Shouldn't be too long now, he's gone, 360
Sixteen inches across, 95
"Slips" he always called them, 133
so much depended, 70
Soap-scented, shiny by the lamp, 159
solitary walk, 30
Solomon Kane, 120
Somebody wise once said, 92
Somehow, in Picasso's "Madman", 208
Something had left me waiting, 324
Sometimes I imagine you, 23
Somewhere at a lane's end, 234
Somewhere in that summer vortex, 352

Somewhere in the lore of long ago, 155
South-West Brook is loud tonight, 363
Summer was, 351
Sun on boarded windows, 172
sun on whorl, 191
sunlight on the wing, 211
suspended, 371

Take what you can, 220
The harbour, 350
The world stayed, 131
The grove, 72
The island's last families, 313
The mailman, buoyant, chirpy soul, 101
The oats lean seaward, 252
The oil-soaked carcass, 240
The scene seems medieval now, 140
The widow, Flora Livingstone, 206
There he was, 253
There was once a saw-mill here, 173
There's a plain old house on a coast, 305
They are passing by, low again, 221
They laughed at this simple girl, 189
They said Xantippe was a shrew, 129
They were two young lovers, 255
This has existential implications. Seriously, such negligible, 59
Thomas Hardy, 42
Three crows drift across the sky, 307
Tommy, the hermit, 20
Tonight, while politicians, 130
Twelfth Night, a sad time, 71

Up here on the dark north wind, 353

Waking before dawn, 193
We could never regard him as one of us, 304
We fished all through the night, 312
We found no keeper at the light, 302
We knew the loon's four calls, 76

We laughed at him then, 177
We were walking alone, 309
West Country cemetery, 364
What if the Beothuk are not all dead, 354
When Charlie Darwin went to sea, 91
When morning breaks, 97
When old birches bend leafless, 311
When the plains were lush, 329
Who could be, 28
wind in the beams, 178
With summer gone, 116
with Suzanne, 64

Years ago, before I knew, 35
You must notice, 346
Your nurse whispered, 56

INDEX OF TITLES

Abandoned Outport, 172
After Georgia O'Keeffe, 40
After Rain, 46
After the Storm, 108
Alders, 229
All to Ourselves, 83
Along that Coast, 261
Angler, The, 310
Apparition, 343
Aquarius, 24
Asters, 116
At L'Anse aux Meadows, 25
At Western Arm, 173

Babel, 329
Back Road, 217
Ballad of Flora, The, 206
Beach Moments, September '56, 271
Bear, The, 179
Bess, 86
Birds and Poets, 42
Birth Control, 326
Bitch, 232
Boatman, 165
Bogey Man, The, 156
Bonfire, 27
Bonfire Night, 205
Bridge, The, 269
By the Tracks, 325

Caligula's Horse, 124
Calling the Children, 234

Cape Shore Woman, 193
Caretaker, 167
Cat Poem, 98
Cellar, The, 300
Charlie Brown, 28
Child on Michaelmas, 114
Children from Porlock, 347
Children in the Alley, 327
Christmas Eve, 30
Circus, 31
Coffin Maker, 95
Communion, 182
Connections, 311
Consecration, A, 201
Country Song, 33
Cowboys, 110
Crows, 34

Day in '45, A, 169
Daedalus, 235
Daedalus at Garden Wall, 238
Dark Morning, 174
Darwin, 91
Dead Boy, The, 170
Devil, 35
Devil at the Dance, 155
Dog-Fish Summer, 337
Dreaming of an Almost Forgotten Friend, 309

Edwardians (Old Photograph), 216
Elsewhere: A Poem to Emily, 92
Evening, Bareneed, Conception Bay, 183
Evening, Signal Hill, 353

Fairy Tale, A, 149
Family, 62
Far Island, The, 249
Farewell to Arms, A, 346
Feathers, 344

February Window, 38
Figures from Ancestral Landscape, 178
Final, 37
Flea, 102
Florence Hardy, 23
Fogscape, 142
French Shore Man, The, 203
Frog-Prince, 100
From the Lighthouse, 302

Ghosts, 247
Ghost Story, 43
Gnostic, 97
Goat and Apple Tree, 140
God's Dog, 73
Grand Canyon, 55
Grove, The, 72
Guitar Player, The, 259
Gulls and Ice, 350

Haiku (1), 210
Haiku (2), 211
Haiku (3), 212
Haiku (4), 213
Haiku (5), 214
Haiku Selections, 364
Hansel and Grethel, 112
Hawk Song, 48
Headland, The, 272
Hermit, 130
Hide and Seek, 241
Hobo Bill, 126
House on the Coast, 305

If Sonnets Were in Fashion, 224
In a Small Cove, 202
In Hardy Country, 147
In Picasso's "Madman", 208
In the Happily Ever After, 49

In the Heart of the Country, 358
In There Somewhere, 354
Interval, 252
Inuk, 283
Ishmael, 301
Ishmael Remembers, 266
Ishmael Remembers (2), 267
Island Woman, 44

Jacob, 54

Last House, The, 139
Last Keeper, The, 135
Leah, 360
Little Man, The, 328
Loon, 76
Lot's Wife, 121
Low Tide, 274

Madonna, The, 313
Make-and-Break, 57
Man of Letters, 101
Marsh, 191
Methodists, 230
Monday Morning, 349
Mummer, The, 175
My Cat in Noah's Ark, 99

Naked Man, The, 185
Nero, 123
New Year's Morning, 2000, 131
Night Class, 45
Noah, 304
North Light, 68

Of Mice and Books, 51
Old Believer, 60
Old Man and the Moon, The, 177
On Cuslett Brook (1979), 215
On Learning that We Share 99% of Our DNA with Lettuce, 59

On Small Island, 164
On the Full Tide, 356
Once After Sunday, 277
Once by the Atlantic, 253
One Fall Night, 162
Only the Wind, 56
Ottawa October Crisis, 1970, 348
Otters on All Soul's Day, 75
Outport Christmas, 163

Pages, 128
Path's End, 66
Pegasus, 61
Peggy, 189
Peppermint Rock, 160
Pilgrim, 65
Poor Peter, 275
Potato Ground, The, 250

Remembering Leonard, 64
Riddle, 151
Riggs, 105

Salmon, 107
Saltbox House, 118
Sandpiper, 223
Santa Fe Trail, 67
Scape, 303
Scarecrow, 306
Sculpin, The, 333
Scythe, The, 255
Seabird, 240
Searching for Ancestors, 78
Second Wife, The, 137
Shop, The, 103
Signs, The, 363
Slips, 133
Snow-Poem Suggestion, 345
Sole Survivor, 362

Solomon Kane, 120
Solstice, Outport Childhood, 158
Something Gone, 324
Stage, 198
Still Life, 153
Storm Coming, Winter Afternoon, 307
Stranger, The, 263
Stranger at Hemlock Cove, 289
"Struggle Into Light": A Poem to John Clare, 226
Summer of Forty Something-or-Other, 352
Summerplace, 171
Summer Was, 351

Tea Room, 109
Thoreau, 89
Three in the Summer Afternoon, 265
To a Poet, 278
To Mary Oliver, 21
To William Carlos Williams, 70
Tommy, 20
Top of the World, 199
Trapper, The, 298
Trek, 19
Trip, 312
Twelfth Night, 71

Uncle, 159

Veteran (1), The, 219
Veteran (2), The, 220
Veteran (3), The, 273
Viking Site, 69
Visitation, 22
Vivaldi, 41
Vortex, 192

Watcher, The, 184
Watercourse, 47
Way, The, 39

White Horses, 258
Widow and the Butcher Boy, The, 187
Wild Geese, 221
Witness, 26

Xantippe, 129

TOM DAWE was born in Long Pond/Manuels, Conception Bay, Newfoundland. He has worked as a high-school teacher, professor of English, visual artist, editor, writer, and poet. He is the author of eighteen books, including poetry, fiction, dramatic script, folklore, and children's literature.

In the seventies, during the Newfoundland "renaissance," he was one of the original founders of Breakwater Books, one of the founding editors of *TickleAce*, and the prose editor of *The Livyere*, a folklore journal. He also worked on *Scruncheons*, a creative-writing journal at Memorial University, and helped organize some of the first poetry readings on campus.

In 2010, he was appointed Poet Laureate of the City of St. John's. In 2011, he was appointed a Member of The Order of Canada, and in the following year, he was awarded The Order of Newfoundland and Labrador. He lives in Conception Bay South.